STAR SONG

AND OTHER ONE-ACT PLAYS

By FLORENCE RYERSON

STAR SONG AND OTHER ONE-ACT PLAYS

Star Song

AND OTHER ONE-ACT PLAYS

by

Florence Ryerson

SAMUEL FRENCH

New York   *Toronto*   *Hollywood*

1951

STAR SONG AND OTHER ONE-ACT PLAYS

ALL RIGHTS RESERVED

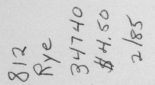
PRINTED IN THE UNITED STATES OF AMERICA
BY THE VAIL-BALLOU PRESS, INC., BINGHAMTON, N. Y.

For

HAL AND MARY RYERSON

CONTENTS

STAR SONG

A Christmas Play in One Act

BY

FLORENCE RYERSON

CHARACTERS

GAIUS, *a Roman soldier*
LUCIUS, *another soldier*
TIRZA, *mistress of the inn*
RACHEL, *a traveler from the North*
AROD, *her husband*
BARSHAN, *owner of a caravan*
NUNA, *a small slave girl*
OCTAVIA, *widow of a Roman general*
SITI, *her Ethiopian slave*

For tableau and procession (optional): MARY, JOSEPH, SHEPHERDS, WISE MEN, PILGRIMS, TOWNSFOLK, etc.

TIME

A mid-winter night in the time of Caesar Augustus.

SCENE

Inner chamber off the main room of an Inn near Bethlehem.

NOTE

The following scenes must be played with the greatest simplicity and naturalness. There is no reason to believe that the guests at the little Inn near Bethlehem on that long-ago winter night had any idea that a great and holy event was in the making.

Undoubtedly they were ordinary wayfarers preoccupied with personal worries which were not so different from those of today. Unless this feeling of naturalness is achieved the play will lose much of its impact.

If a simpler production is preferred the final procession may be eliminated and the curtain brought down after Octavia's last speech, or the Nativity tableau may be used without the procession.

STAR SONG

The inner room of a small inn near Bethlehem is a crude chamber with a door at Right which leads into the main room, double doors in the upper wall Center, a deep window with shutters at Left. The furniture consists of a few rough stools, one long bench, an iron brasier. Except for a greenish distemper where the plaster is peeling, the walls are a dull white. The only color in the room comes from a scarlet mantle thrown across one end of the bench.

At Rise: GAIUS *and* LUCIUS, *two Roman centurions, are playing darts against the Right wall, above the main door.* GAIUS *is a typical hard-boiled man of war.* LUCIUS *is younger, better-looking, the owner of the mantle.*

GAIUS. [*As* LUCIUS *throws.*] A miss—and a miss—and a miss! Your wristlet is mine!

LUCIUS. By Janus, the darts are bewitched! [*Taking off wristlet and handing it over.*] Here—

GAIUS. I'll play you for the other. This one is lonely without its mate.

LUCIUS. Its mate will soon have it back again!

GAIUS. That we shall see! [*Crosses down to door and opens it.*] Ho!—you—out there! We want wine! Wine!

TIRZA. [*Off—in a shrill voice.*] Kick those dogs out the door—do you hear me? I said, kick them out!

LUCIUS. [*Chuckling.*] The mistress of the inn is in fine form tonight.

GAIUS. And why not? With the travelers pouring in she stands to make a pot of gold.

LUCIUS. Two pots—or she'll skin them!

TIRZA. [*Still off, but coming nearer.*] Throw more wood on the fire! Tell those shepherds to keep their dirty hands out of the stew! [*In a pleasanter tone.*] This way—mind that step! Now, through this door— [*She enters, a grasping shrew of a woman, hard as nails, with a tight-lipped mouth and darting eyes. She is followed by* RACHEL, *also a domineering type.* RACHEL'S *husband,* AROD, *a gentle, apologetic little man brings up the rear. Both the travelers are over middle-age.* RACHEL *carries a saddle-bag packed to bursting,* AROD *a bed-roll of rugs and blankets.*] Here you are! The best accommodations in the house.

RACHEL. [*Looking around scornfully.*] You don't expect us to sleep here!

TIRZA. And why not? It's a fine room! A beautiful room! Clean and dry and convenient!

RACHEL. Convenient to the pig-sty!

AROD. Now, Rachel—

RACHEL. [*At window.*] Why, those are cattle out there. I can see oxen—and sheep—

TIRZA. They'll not be here long. Some shepherds are just passing through.

RACHEL. An inn for shepherds! [*To her husband.*] I told you we should keep on into Bethlehem.

AROD. [*Warningly.*] We heard that the inns were all full, Rachel.

TIRZA. Full to bursting, but don't let that stop you! There's a place below—only two or three miles—that's used for butchering cattle. I understand they are renting out stalls for the night.

AROD. No! No! I'm sure this will do nicely. Won't it, Rachel?

RACHEL. [*Ungraciously.*] If it's all we can get it'll have to do. What about those centurions?

GAIUS. [*Grinning.*] We go with the room, lady.

TIRZA. I forgot to mention—you'll have to share floor space.

RACHEL. With *men?*

TIRZA. Oh, there'll be a woman, too. I'm expecting a couple from Nazareth.

RACHEL. Really—

TIRZA. [*Without stopping.*] You couldn't expect a whole room to yourself—not with crowds coming in for the census. You can spread your bed there—to the left of the brasier.

GAIUS. [*As* RACHEL *looks at him suspiciously.*] Don't worry about me, Gramma. I'll put my spear up—so.

LUCIUS. And I'll put mine—so.

GAIUS. We'll keep on our side—if you'll keep on yours.

RACHEL. Insolence! [*Shouting and clattering sounds from off Left.*] What's that noise?

AROD. [*At window.*] Another caravan is arriving.

TIRZA. Let me look! [*Pushes him roughly aside.*] I recognize that lead camel! And the rider, too! It's Barshan the Goshenite!

AROD. Barshan!

TIRZA. Back from Egypt.

RACHEL. That thieving jackal!

TIRZA. I see you know him.

RACHEL. Know him!

AROD. He sold me a bill of sandalwood once.

RACHEL. Pinewood you mean! Pine with sandal-oil dropped into the worm-holes.

TIRZA. [*Crossing to door Right.*] That's Barshan, for sure. He's an artful rogue. But when he tries to gammon me with his trader's tricks he meets his match!

LUCIUS. We believe you!

GAIUS. [*Calling after her as she leaves.*] Hey—send in that wine!

RACHEL. [*Who has been looking around—to* AROD.] A hole! That's what it is—an abominable rat-hole! I told you we should never have left the North!

AROD. But Rachel, we had no choice.

LUCIUS. You are Northern folk?

AROD. From Lebanon these days. We came originally from—

RACHEL. [*As usual, riding over him rough-shod.*] Just outside of Bethlehem. We've settled in the North for the sake of my husband's business.

AROD. I'm a dealer in—

RACHEL. He's a dealer in woods. We have a nice little business, or did have. Heaven knows what will become of it whilst we're gone on this journey, but *he* insisted upon coming—

AROD. What else could I do when Caesar commanded?

RACHEL. Caesar, Caesar, always Caesar! "I want a census," he says. "I want to count the whole world."

AROD. [*One eye on the* CENTURIONS.] Now, Rachel—

RACHEL. He couldn't count us where we were, oh, no! We had to drop everything and go back where we came from, leaving house and business and my bit of garden. I'd like to know who's going to water my garden whilst I'm gone! Not Caesar, I'll be bound! [*Turns on* AROD, *who is tugging at her sleeve.*] And don't you stick up for him!

AROD. [*Meekly.*] I'm not sticking up for him. I'm just saying that—Caesar is Caesar. He has the power to give orders.

GAIUS. Don't you wish *you* had?

[*Laughs, whacks him on the back, crosses to door and throws it open.* TIRZA *and* BARSHAN *can be heard shouting at each other as they bargain.*]

TIRZA. [*Off.*] Seven bales of straw, two of fodder, bread, sixty loaves, and not a crumb more.

BARSHAN. [*Off.*] With parched corn and lentils for twenty men.

RACHEL. That's Barshan's voice.

TIRZA. [*Off.*] Twenty men! Do you want to ruin me?

GAIUS. She's holding her own! [*Calls off.*] Mistress! Where's that wine?

TIRZA. [*Off.*] Coming! Do you think I have wings on my feet?

GAIUS. You'll have a sword in your gizzard if you don't bring it soon. [*To* OTHERS.] The old wild-cat!

BARSHAN. [*Off.*] Three sheep and one calf, five cheeses and fifty oil cakes.

TIRZA. [*Off.*] No oil cakes! [*She enters, carrying a flagon of wine and two goblets.*]

[*She is followed by* BARSHAN, *a middle-aged man with a thin, cruel face.*]

BARSHAN. I must have oil cakes!

TIRZA. Perhaps you'd like cakes of gold and silver—or mother-of-pearl set with lapis.

BARSHAN. At the price you are charging you could serve diamonds!

LUCIUS. [*A quick exchange with* GAIUS.] Jackal against wild-cat!

GAIUS. Your wristlet on the cat.

LUCIUS. [*Indicating second wristlet.*] This on the jackal.

TIRZA. [*Whining.*] Would you rob a poor widow? Every penny I make is squeezed from the marrow of my bones.

BARSHAN. And the bones of the travelers forced to stay in this flea-trap.

TIRZA. Flea-trap! I'd have you know the greatest have stopped here!

BARSHAN. Stopped, but not stayed. One whiff—they passed on.

LUCIUS. [*To* GAIUS.] First blood to the jackal.

TIRZA. Why not pass on yourself, Egyptian? Find place at other inns which smell sweeter—you, with your dirty men and stinking camels!

BARSHAN. [*Quickly.*] I was but jesting. Cannot you take a little jest?

GAIUS. [*To* LUCIUS.] Second blood to the wild-cat.

BARSHAN. [*Calling out window.*] Hey, you there! No, not you—I want Nuna. Fetch my bed-roll and my basin.

TIRZA. Not here. The bargain we made was for shelter in the cattle-sheds.

BARSHAN. For my men. Not for me. I sleep within.

TIRZA. I have no place for you within. The big room out there is jammed to the doors. I've sold the last space in here.

RACHEL. And no snake is going to steal it from us!

BARSHAN. I know that voice! [*Turns around to grin at* AROD *and* RACHEL.] How goes the wood business?

AROD. Well enough.

RACHEL. While the thieves were in Egypt. Look you—this is our space— [*She starts rapidly unpacking her bed-roll and other possessions and laying them out at Left.*]

LUCIUS. [*As* BARSHAN *looks toward the Right.*] And ours—from here to here—marked by our spears.

GAIUS. Which might turn in the wrong direction if disturbed.

BARSHAN. There is space between.

AROD. That is promised to a couple from Nazareth.

TIRZA. The man sent word ahead that they must be warm. The woman is near her time.

BARSHAN. A woman near her time should remain at home.

RACHEL. Not when Caesar calls for a census.

TIRZA. [*Persuasively.*] But there is still a sweet bit of floor in the threshing house. Only ten in there—all nice clean shepherds—and I planned for twelve. [*As* BARSHAN *snarls his disgust.*] Or the cow-shed, now. It's a beautiful cow-shed. The roof is quite whole. Scarce a leak in it.

BARSHAN. [*Craftily.*] Has it walls all around?

TIRZA. All around. Look you—one wall is the side of this house. Those doors lead into it.

BARSHAN. So the warmth from this room can be felt through the wall?

TIRZA. Yes—yes. And there's a brasier with charcoal—and fresh straw laid on the floor.

GAIUS. [*Grinning.*] Fit for a king!

TIRZA. Fit for a king!

BARSHAN. Or a pair of Nazarenes.

RACHEL. For shame!

BARSHAN. How much better for a woman nearing her time

to have a quiet retreat with no one to disturb her—rather than a noisy spot like this—

TIRZA. But I have taken money. The man sent the price—not an hour since.

BARSHAN. And I sent the price—yesterday.

TIRZA. How's that?

BARSHAN. By one of my drivers. You haven't forgotten!

TIRZA. [Meaningly.] It might help me to remember if I saw the money—

BARSHAN. [Hastily.] I didn't pay in silver. I paid in the best—

RACHEL. [Cutting in.] Sandalwood.

BARSHAN. [Ignoring her.] Spices. And a length of Egyptian cloth. Surely you remember the Egyptian cloth—thin as mist —most beautifully patterned—worth its weight in gold.

[NUNA enters from Right, staggering under an enormous roll of rugs. She is so concealed by her burden it is impossible to see anything except one hand which carries a wash basin.]

NUNA. Master, your bed-roll.

BARSHAN. [Turning.] Eh? Oh, Nuna. Spread it on the floor.

TIRZA. Not on this floor! Give me my money or you sleep with your camels—and pay over quickly. I've the work of three women waiting for me.

BARSHAN. The work of three— [Has a sudden idea.] What you need is a slave. A fine female slave to lighten your labor. As it happens I've brought one from Egypt—

TIRZA. I've tried your Egyptians: lazy dogs. I wore out ten whips on the back of the last one!

BARSHAN. This is not an Egyptian. Her mother was a Greek—her father also.

TIRZA. Greek—eh? [*Grudgingly.*] The Greeks are not so bad. I've had Greeks I could work like horses—until they dropped.

BARSHAN. Then it's a bargain! [*To* NUNA.] Bring those here.

TIRZA. Not so fast! First I must see your slave.

BARSHAN. That you shall. [*Lifts bed-roll from* NUNA, *disclosing a thin, big-eyed child of twelve, obviously terrified.*] Here she is.

TIRZA. That—mosquito?

[*The* CHILD *shrinks into herself as they laugh.*]

BARSHAN. She's a trifle thin now because of the journey. She'll fatten quickly and grow strong. Already she can carry wood and water—

TIRZA. To carry straw would be too much for her! Look at those arms—like reeds! And her legs are— [*A closer look.*] Why—the creature is lame!

BARSHAN. Only a little.

TIRZA. A little! Walk, girl. [NUNA *hesitates, looking fearfully at* BARSHAN. TIRZA *makes a threatening gesture.*] I said *walk!* [NUNA *limps a few steps.*] Fah! She stumbles like a hobbled colt.

BARSHAN. She is shamming. Pretending to be more lame than she is because she doesn't want to leave the caravan— [*Grabs* NUNA *by the arm.*] We've been so kind, you don't want to leave us. That's true, isn't it? Isn't it, Nuna?

NUNA. [*Shows he is hurting her.*] Yes—yes, Master.

BARSHAN. [*Releasing her arm.*] Look at her! The brightest hand-maid I've ever had to offer! And of good blood. The best. Tell her about your people, Nuna. [*As* NUNA *shrinks away again.*] Tell her!

NUNA. [*At first faintly, then with growing pride.*] My mother was a lady from Tarsus. A beautiful lady—very good and kind, my father owned ships.

BARSHAN. Many ships!

TIRZA. A fleet, no doubt!

[*A* SHEPHERDS' CHORUS *begins singing very softly in the distance—all male voices.*]

NUNA. [*Missing the sarcasm.*] Yes. A fleet of ships. One summer we went for a trip on the water—a lovely trip to Cypress where we had another home.

BARSHAN. A great house full of slaves—

NUNA. No! No! That was in Tarsus. This was a little house, just big enough for the three of us. My father would fetch the wood and my mother would cook. We were so happy that summer. So happy— [*A little catch of the breath.*] But on the way home, pirates came down on us. They captured our ship and killed my father. They planned to take us to Egypt and sell us, but on the way my mother—

TIRZA. [*As the* CHILD *hesitates.*] Well, go on!

NUNA. A sickness struck the ship. My mother died, and I—I— [*She breaks off with a sob.*]

BARSHAN. She was left with the lameness.

AROD. Poor child.

TIRZA. [*Drily, to* BARSHAN.] Very tragic and well told. I see you've coached her carefully in her lies.

BARSHAN. They are no lies. She has lived in our house a year. My wife says a cleverer child or one more eager to learn she has never seen.

TIRZA. Yet she was willing to part with this treasure. Why?

BARSHAN. [*A trifle shame-faced.*] It was because of the sands. My wife reads the future in the sands.

TIRZA. A sorceress!

BARSHAN. No! No! Only for her own amusement. The sands told her—oh, I cannot speak of such foolishness! [*To* NUNA.] Tell what the sands foretold.

NUNA. They said if my master would carry me to Bethlehem, I would bring him a treasure more precious than gold.

GAIUS. Bed space for the night! Ho! That *is* a treasure!

BARSHAN. I did not say I believed, though I will admit we had the quickest trip up from Egypt I have had in my lifetime. The camels seemed to fly and they needed no guiding.

NUNA. They were following the star.

[*The choral* MUSIC *swells a trifle but is still distant.*]

AROD. [*Gently.*] What star, child?

NUNA. Why, the great white star. The one that was always in the sky just ahead.

BARSHAN. Always talking about that star! None of us saw anything but she was so sure she almost persuaded us into seeing.

AROD. A star! I remember whilst we were on our way we met a caravan—

RACHEL. [*Again breaking in on him.*] With three wise men. Traveling like kings, they were, with slaves and tents and jewels ablazing. They said they were coming to do homage to some prince—

AROD. [*Cutting in eagerly.*] And a star would disclose his abiding place.

BARSHAN. Did you *see* the star?

RACHEL. Not I!

TIRZA. Now that is a strange thing. Shepherds have been coming in all evening from the hills. They talk about a star which they say is overhead—a great white wonder—like a diamond in the sky.

NUNA. It *is* like a diamond! [*Crosses to window, throws the shutters open.*] Look! Up there!

[*They cross to window, look out.*]

RACHEL. I see only storm clouds.

BARSHAN. Above the black hills.

NUNA. But you must see the light! Surely you can see it!

LUCIUS. I see only the light of the shepherds' campfires.

TIRZA. [*Roughly to* NUNA.] What are you trying to do? Make us all star-struck so that you can get out of work? You'll soon forget your star-gazing here!

BARSHAN. [*Delighted.*] Then the bargain is made? You'll keep the child?

TIRZA. It's no bargain for me, but I'm short of help, so—

BARSHAN. Agreed! If she doesn't give satisfaction I'll guarantee to take her off your hands.

TIRZA. [*She really means it.*] If she doesn't give satisfaction *I'll* guarantee to take it out of her hide.

GAIUS. And the marrow of her bones! [*He laughs loudly.*]

[SHEPHERDS' MUSIC *comes to an end.*]

TIRZA. [*Sharply to* NUNA.] Step lively, now! Close that window! Fetch a basket of charcoal for the brasier! [*As* NUNA *blunders toward the Right.*] Not that way, fool! Through the cow-shed. And be quick about it!

NUNA. Yes, mistress. [*Exits through Center doors.*]

LUCIUS. The jackal wins! I'll trouble you for that wristlet.

GAIUS. Not so fast—

BARSHAN. [*To* TIRZA *who is, apparently, looking around for something.*] Out of the way, woman! I must spread my bed.

TIRZA. Not until I have found them—

BARSHAN. Them?

TIRZA. [*More searching.*] Those spices you sent me and the cloth from Egypt.

BARSHAN. [*Outraged.*] *What?*

TIRZA. Surely you've not forgotten the cloth like mist—most beautifully patterned—

BARSHAN. You expect spices and cloth after my giving you the girl?

TIRZA. Who said it was *after?* You sent the spices and cloth *yesterday*—remember?

BARSHAN. By the Bulls of Belial! Never have I seen such a scurvy skinflint!

NUNA. [*Hurrying back in on cue 'scurvy.'*] Mistress! Mistress! Two travelers have arrived. He says I am to tell you, Joseph son of Jacob, from Nazareth.

TIRZA. [*Her eyes on* BARSHAN.] The Nazarenes.

NUNA. He says he sent payment ahead.

TIRZA. So he did. In hard silver. Take up those rags—[*Indicates* BARSHAN's *bed.*]—throw them outside.

BARSHAN. [*Capitulating.*] No. wait! [*To* NUNA.] Tell my men to bring in a length of Egyptian cloth—and a measure of spice.

TIRZA. Two measures!

BARSHAN. [*Resignedly.*] Tell them two measures.

TIRZA. I'll tell them myself. And the spice will be weighed on *my* scales—*not yours!*

GAIUS. [*As she goes toward door.*] Victory to the wild-cat!

NUNA. [*Bewildered, takes a few steps after* TIRZA.] Mistress—the travelers from Nazareth!

TIRZA. There's naught left but the cow-shed. They'll have to make do with that.

NUNA. But the lady is ill. She needs some place to rest.

TIRZA. [*Shrugs.*] Let her rest in the straw! [*She goes out Right.*]

BARSHAN. [*Harshly, as* NUNA *still hesitates.*] You heard your mistress. Show the Nazarenes into the cow-shed.

RACHEL. [*Calling after her as she leaves by Center door.*] And bring in that charcoal!

GAIUS. [*To* LUCIUS, *who is handing over the second wristlet.*] Will you have revenge? The wristlets against your mantle.

LUCIUS. Not my mantle. My ring—but not my mantle.

AROD. It is a fine garment.

RACHEL. Warm and well woven.

BARSHAN. I could use such a mantle in my travels. Will ye part with it, soldier?

LUCIUS. Never! I got it from an old witch-woman in Joppa. She told me it would bring me the greatest moment of my life.

AROD. And how will you know the greatest moment when it comes?

LUCIUS. That she forgot to tell. But, in the meantime—it serves to keep me warm.

RACHEL. [*Fretfully.*] You'll have need of it tonight! There's a draft from the window which fair freezes my blood. [*To* AROD.] Move that brasier this way.

BARSHAN. No, by Astaroth! I bought this space beside it for ten times it's worth and I mean to—

RACHEL. [*Cutting in on cue "worth."*] You bought the *space*. Naught was said about the brasier.

BARSHAN. Nevertheless—the brasier stays where it is!

GAIUS. [*Solemnly to* LUCIUS.] You hear the Egyptian?

LUCIUS. [*Equally solemnly.*] The brasier stays where it is.

GAIUS. That's what he says!

[*The two proceed to take the brasier between them and carry it toward their own space, Right.*]

RACHEL. You leave that alone! Arod—stop them!

AROD. Now, Rachel—please!

BARSHAN. Put that down! You hear me? Put it down! ⎫ [*Together.*]

LUCIUS. Careful! You're invading Roman territory!

BARSHAN. I've paid to sleep warm, and by the tomb of my fathers I mean to do so!

GAIUS. [*Threatening him with spear.*] Swear by your own tomb, Egypt!

LUCIUS. You're heading there fast! [*Gives him a shove which throws him over at Left among* RACHEL'S *possessions.*]

RACHEL. [*Furiously.*] Go 'way! Get out! This is our space!

BARSHAN. Quiet, you beldam! [*Starts back toward the* CEN-

TURIONS. [*From now on all talk more or less at once in a babble of angry voices.*] You Roman dogs! Lay hands on me again and I'll show you who I am!

RACHEL. Beldam! [*To* AROD.] Did you hear what he called me? Beldam!

BARSHAN. I'll appeal to Herod! He'll send your names to Caesar! You'll be thrown to the buzzards!

RACHEL. [*Still to* BARSHAN.] You're a thief and a liar and dirt is too good for you.

LUCIUS. That's the way, Gramma! Go it!
AROD. Hush, Rachel! Hush! } [*Together.*]

RACHEL. [*Runs to door, Right, calling.*] Mistress! Mistress Tirza!
GAIUS. [*To* BARSHAN.] One more word out of you and I'll run you through the gullet! } [*Together.*]

AROD. Now, gentlemen, please! Please, gentlemen! Let us be peaceable!

BARSHAN. Keep out of this!
GAIUS. Quiet, you fly-speck! } [*Together, roaring at him.*]

TIRZA. [*Hurrying into the room.*] What's amiss here?

BARSHAN. Those cut-throats took the brasier. They wish to freeze me!
RACHEL. The thief trampled on our things! Keep him out of our space!
AROD. If you would help us settle the matter quietly— } [*Together.*]

LUCIUS. That jackal insulted the army!

GAIUS. We'll denounce you to the Governor
for harboring traitors!

> [*Together.*]

TIRZA. Hush! Hold your tongues! You sound like dogs fighting— [*As they continue to complain, ad lib.*] Quiet! Quiet! [*Seizes spear from* GAIUS, *pounds handle on the floor and yells.*] I will have quiet! [*They* ALL *stop short.*] Now, what is the trouble?

GAIUS. [*Pointing at* BARSHAN.] It's that son of Beelzebub—

RACHEL. He's to blame.

BARSHAN. I but demanded my rights!

AROD. If you would only say—"You sleep here—you here—you here—"

RACHEL. No matter what she says, I sleep *here!*

BARSHAN. And I *here!*

TIRZA. None of you sleeps here.

LUCIUS. What?

GAIUS. How's that?

RACHEL. What did you say?

AROD. Not sleep here!

BARSHAN. Another trick!

> [*Together.*]

TIRZA. A new guest has arrived. A lady of great importance. I must have the room for her.

[ALL *break out again.*]

RACHEL. Great importance, indeed! We're important, too, I'll have you know!

AROD. We've paid our money—

BARSHAN. We have our rights!

GAIUS. The army has preference.

TIRZA. Assuredly. That is why I require the room. The lady is the widow of your late general.

LUCIUS. [*Startled.*] Octavia?

GAIUS. Octavia here?

RACHEL. Who is Octavia?

GAIUS. [*Rapidly gathering up his things while* LUCIUS *does the same.*] If you are wise—you won't wait to find out.

BARSHAN. No woman is going to drive me out!

RACHEL. Nor me, neither!

TIRZA. Hush!

[OCTAVIA *enters, Right, followed by part of her retinue. She is tall, graceful, coldly beautiful and immediately dominates the scene.* SITI, *her personal slave-maid, is a middle-aged Ethiopian, warm and kindly. She is directing* TWO BEARERS *who carry painted chests and bundles tied in bright silks, and* TWO SLAVES *who carry* OCTAVIA'S *chair. This is almost a small throne made of gilt wood picked out in color, with brilliant cushions. For a moment* OCTAVIA *stands looking about her. She ignores the other occupants as though they are furniture.*]

TIRZA. [*Humbly.*] I know it is a poor room, your ladyship, very small and mean. Quite unworthy of your occupancy—

OCTAVIA. It is the best you have to offer?

TIRZA. It is *all* I have to offer. I'm sure your ladyship would be more comfortable in one of the larger inns near the center of town—

OCTAVIA. [*Firmly.*] I wish to stay here. What is through that door?

TIRZA. Only a cow-shed.

OCTAVIA. It will do for my slaves.

TIRZA. I'm sorry, but it is already occupied. A Nazarene couple. The woman is— [*Whispers the rest of the information.*]

OCTAVIA. Very well. So long as she does not disturb me— they may remain. [*A wave of the hand toward the belongings of the* OTHERS *which subtly includes the people themselves.*] Clear away this rubbish.

TIRZA. At once, your ladyship! [*To the* OTHERS.] Get your things out of here—and be quick about it!

RACHEL. But where are we to go?

TIRZA. I'll make space for you somehow in the outer room— unless you'd prefer the threshing-house floor?

RACHEL. No! No! [*To* AROD, *pushing the bedding into his arms.*] Go hold the space. I'll bring the rest.

AROD. Yes, Rachel. [*He goes out, humbling himself before* OCTAVIA *as he passes her.*]

[SITI *helps* OCTAVIA *to remove her long mantle, disclosing a rich dress.*]

TIRZA. Your ladyship's slaves may sleep in the threshing

house— [*To* BARSHAN.] And you with them. As for you Romans—

OCTAVIA. The soldiers seem clean and not ill-favored. Let them guard the door.

GAIUS AND LUCIUS. Yes, my lady.

[*They salute and go out with the* SLAVES *and* BARSHAN *who darts furious glances at* TIRZA.]

OCTAVIA. [*To* SITI, *as she moves toward her chair.*] Unpack my things. And tell that woman if her wine is not too bad she may send in a flagon.

TIRZA. My very best, your ladyship. And perhaps some fried cakes? I'm said to have a fine hand with fried cakes.

OCTAVIA. [*Shuddering.*] Spare me! Wine only. My slaves will prepare my food. [*To* SITI, *with a contemptuous glance toward* RACHEL, *who is trying to pack her things into bundles but is so nervous she keeps dropping them.*] Quick! Bring me some perfume! This room reeks of those cattle.

SITI. Here, my lady.

[OCTAVIA *takes the small flask, sinks into her chair with her eyes closed. This brings her with her back toward the Center doors so that she does not see* NUNA *who comes in with a large basket of charcoal. The doors are difficult for her to manage. She makes some noise in closing them.*]

OCTAVIA. [*Angrily.*] Who dares break in like that?

TIRZA. Quiet, you clod! It is the charcoal for the fire, my lady.

OCTAVIA. Good. It is cold in here.

[SHEPHERDS' CHORUS *begins singing again—very softly.*]

TIRZA. Cold? Your ladyship is cold? [*To* NUNA.] Bring the basket here. Not there—here! Now go fetch the other brasier from the cow-shed.

NUNA. But the guest from Nazareth is using it to heat water for the lady.

TIRZA. The lady! Why do you call her a lady? They are humble folk. He is only a carpenter.

NUNA. But she *is* a lady. So gentle and sweet—and beautiful—you should see how beautiful she is.

TIRZA. I've no time for looking now.

NUNA. But she needs help, mistress. There is no woman with her and she needs help so terribly.

SITI. I should be glad to help her. [*To* OCTAVIA.] You know I have understanding of such things.

OCTAVIA. [*Crisply.*] I have need of you here.

NUNA. [*Timidly, to* TIRZA.] Then—may I help her, mistress? For only a little while?

TIRZA. Not with all the fetching and carrying there is to be done!

RACHEL. [*Suddenly stands erect. Speaks to* NUNA *quietly, firmly, with a certain dignity.*] I will help your lady.

NUNA. [*Almost sobbing in relief.*] Oh—thank you.

[SHEPHERDS' CHORUS *swells.*]

RACHEL. [*Opens Center doors, looks into room beyond, stops in surprise—speaks softly.*] She *is* beautiful. And young. So young! [*She exits, closing doors.*]

TIRZA. [*To* NUNA, *as though breaking a spell.*] Don't stand there gaping! Go fetch that brasier.

OCTAVIA. No, this one is sufficient, but I should like some warm water to wash my hands.

TIRZA. At once, my lady! [*To* NUNA.] You heard! Off to the kitchen! Fetch water! [*To* OCTAVIA *again as* NUNA *hurries out Right.*] There! The fire is remade. I'll bring you the wine.

OCTAVIA. Wait!—Who is that singing?

TIRZA. It is the shepherds. If they disturb you I'll have them stopped.

OCTAVIA. No—let them sing. [TIRZA *exits Right.* OCTAVIA *stands by the window, listening, while* SITI *lays out her toilet articles on the bench which she has covered with a bright scarf. After a moment* OCTAVIA *speaks softly, smiling to herself.*] I know that song. The shepherds in the hills above Capua were singing it the day my husband first brought me home as a bride.

SITI. I remember that day, my lady.

OCTAVIA. And do you remember the night my baby was born? It was a night like this—very dark and still. Her hair was pale gold and she had a little dimple here. Everyone said there had never been such a beautiful child.

SITI. I remember.

OCTAVIA. First my husband—and then my baby— [*Her voice breaks. She swings about.*] Do you believe the wise man told the truth? That here, in this Inn, I will be eased of my sorrow?

SITI. I believe that he told the truth, my lady.

OCTAVIA. [*An abrupt change to hardness.*] How much did he pay you to say that? If he was lying I shall have you whipped for bringing me to him. I think I shall have you whipped to death!

SITI. [*Gently, lovingly.*] Will that ease you, my lady?

OCTAVIA. [*Breaking.*] Siti! [SITI *puts her arms about her and comforts her.* NUNA *enters Right.*] Who is that?

NUNA. Just me. Nuna. With the water for your hands.

SITI. Bring it here.

[*She goes to get a basin and striped linen towel while* NUNA *stands near the window, holding the ewer.*]

NUNA. The star is coming nearer every minute.

OCTAVIA. There are no stars tonight. Not one.

NUNA. But there is one. There—almost overhead—

OCTAVIA. You must be dreaming. [*To* SITI.] Do *you* see her star?

SITI. [*Quietly.*] I have seen it for three nights, my lady.

OCTAVIA. [*Angrily.*] You are mocking me! For three nights the sky has been overcast.

NUNA. If you can't see it—surely you can hear the music. Listen!

OCTAVIA. Those are shepherds.

NUNA. No, this is different music—very high and clear— like the voices of angels.

OCTAVIA. [*To* SITI.] Do *you* hear?

SITI. [*Slowly.*] I am not sure—

OCTAVIA. [*Suddenly harsh again, closes the shutters over the window.*] Must I sit here forever while you gabble? Bring me the water for my hands.

[SITI *and* NUNA *hurry to hold the basin and pour the water over her hands.*]

SITI. Here, my lady.

[*As* OCTAVIA *bends, a pendant she is wearing swings out into the light.*]

NUNA. Oh!

OCTAVIA. What is it?

NUNA. Your jewel. It is so beautiful. Why, there is carving on it.

OCTAVIA. [*Showing it to her, not unkindly.*] That is the symbol of eternal life.

NUNA. And on the gold there is sign writing—such as I saw in Egypt.

OCTAVIA. It was found in Egypt—in a royal tomb. The writing says—"I came from a King, to a King I shall return."

NUNA. [*Now very close to her.*] It is lovely. All blue and green—like the sea.

[SHEPHERDS *finish their singing.*]

OCTAVIA. My husband gave it to me when our little girl was born. [*With a sudden change of tone.*] Take your hands away! Do not touch me! [*As* NUNA *starts back, staring.*]

Why should you be alive—a filthy crawling beetle, lame and ugly—when by beautiful child is dead?

SITI. My lady! My lady!

OCTAVIA. Get out of my sight! [*Pushes* NUNA *away so violently the child almost falls, then drops down on the window seat, her head in her arms.*]

SITI. [*Helping* NUNA *to regain her balance.*] You must forgive her. She has suffered so much.

NUNA. [*Softly.*] I forgive her. [*She goes out Right.*]

OCTAVIA. Air! I must have air! [*She pushes the window open and leans out.*] The shepherds have stopped their singing.

SITI. Yes. [*Crossing to her.*] But the child was right—there is still music.

OCTAVIA. I hear nothing. Do you still see the star?

SITI. Yes, my lady. Now it is so close—it seems as though I could reach up and touch it.

[TIRZA *enters with a flagon.*]

OCTAVIA. Music I cannot hear—from a star I cannot see! [*Draws back from window with a shiver.*] Oh, I am cold! Cold!

TIRZA. This wine will warm your ladyship.

SITI. [*Gently.*] Come to the fire. I will bring you a shawl.

OCTAVIA. [*Rises from window, suddenly makes a discovery.*] Where is my amulet?

TIRZA. Your ladyship has lost something?

OCTAVIA. My amulet. The chain is here but the jewel is gone!

TIRZA. It has fallen to the floor, or among the cushions.

SITI. [*Looking about.*] It is not here—nor here—

OCTAVIA. It is nowhere about my dress.

SITI. [*Looking over window seat.*] You were sitting by this window—

TIRZA. You must have lost it on the road before you came.

OCTAVIA. No—I had it in my hand, while I was in that chair. I showed it to the lame slave girl— [*A new thought.*] The slave! She has stolen it!

TIRZA. Nuna?

SITI. Oh, no, mistress! } [*Together.*]

OCTAVIA. She admired the jewel. She said it was beautiful. You heard!

TIRZA. [*Starting Right.*] I'll send for her.

OCTAVIA. Quickly! Quickly!

TIRZA. [*At door, Right.*] Nuna! Nuna! Centurion—have you seen the lame slave girl?

GAIUS. [*Coming to door.*] She passed a moment since.

TIRZA. Find her. Bring her here.

OCTAVIA. It will do no good. She has had time to hide the jewel. She will never tell where it is hidden.

TIRZA. [*Grimly.*] There are ways of making her tell, my lady.

OCTAVIA. Yes, of course. She can be made to tell.

SITI. The child is so young—I cannot believe she would steal—

OCTAVIA. Quiet! [*Suddenly suspicious.*] Or—wait! Why do you say that? Are you, perhaps, in league with her?

SITI. Mistress!

[GAIUS *and* LUCIUS *enter with* NUNA *between them.*]

GAIUS. Here is your starveling.

OCTAVIA. [*Crossing swiftly.*] My amulet! What have you done with my amulet?

NUNA. Amulet?

SITI. The blue and green jewel.

TIRZA. Give it to us!

NUNA. [*Stammering.*] But I cannot!

OCTAVIA. We know you have it—

NUNA. No! No!

OCTAVIA. You were with me there—I have not left the room—

NUNA. I haven't seen your jewel—not since you showed it to me—

TIRZA. That is a lie!

OCTAVIA. You stole it! You've hidden it!

GAIUS. In Rome we strangle thieves.

OCTAVIA. Or crucify them.

LUCIUS. [*Not unkindly.*] Confess, girl, and save yourself.

GAIUS. What have you done with it?

OCTAVIA. Where did you hide it?

[Together.]

TIRZA. [*Picks up leather strap from among* OCTAVIA's *luggage, holds it threateningly.*] Tell us! Tell us!

NUNA. [*Frantic with fear as they all move in on her.*] I haven't your jewel! I swear it by—oh, by what God can I swear? You have so many Gods! Of Egypt—of Rome—your Jewish God! By all of your Gods, I did not take the jewel!

OCTAVIA. I tire of this. Hold her, Centurion.

GAIUS. Yes, my lady.

NUNA. No! No! [*She runs to the Center doors, throws out her arms and beats on them.*] Help me! Save me! Oh, save me!

[*The* CENTURIONS *seize her arms, pulling her downstage from the doors which open slowly, disclosing not darkness as before, but a light so brilliant it is dazzling. This light cuts off the scene beyond and outlines the figure of* RACHEL *who is standing in the opening between the doors. She has thrown a white shawl about her shoulders and a white kerchief over her head. All the lines of petulance have disappeared from her face. During the opening of the doors a new* CHORUS *has begun singing. This is the* CHORUS OF ANGELS *and it is made up largely of women's voices, in contrast to the* MALE CHORUS OF SHEPHERDS. *At first this singing is very soft and far away.*]

RACHEL. [*Putting her finger to her lips.*] Hush! A child has been born to Mary of Nazareth.

NUNA. A baby—

TIRZA. [*In an oddly gentle voice.*] Born in my cow-shed.

RACHEL. A man-child. Very strong and beautiful.

[*The music grows a little louder.*]

OCTAVIA. [*Also with gentleness.*] It is cold out there. You must bring the child in.

SITI. [*Crossing to bench.*] I will make a place for it here—

RACHEL. [*Smiling.*] Mary has already made a place for him. He is cradled in the manger.

OCTAVIA. The manger! Oh, no!

[*She breaks off as* BARSHAN *stumbles into the room, crosses to her, falls on one knee.*]

BARSHAN. Pardon, lady! Forgive me! [*Holding out his hand.*] I am a thief!

OCTAVIA. My amulet!

BARSHAN. You leaned out of the window to look at the sky. I saw it fall to the ground—and I kept it.

OCTAVIA. [*Looking at him, puzzled.*] No one suspected— yet you brought it back. Why?

BARSHAN. I do not know why. When I first took the jewel it was cool and beautiful in my hand. I thought only of the fortune it would bring. Then, suddenly, a star in the heavens burned white—this star in my hand seemed to catch fire. My eyes were filled with light. I saw I must bring the jewel back to you.

GAIUS. And we blamed the girl.

OCTAVIA. Yes. Come here to me, Nuna. Do not be afraid.

[NUNA *comes to her timidly.* OCTAVIA *tips up her face, then suddenly seems to be struck by some thought. She pushes the kerchief up from her forehead. It falls to the ground, disclosing quite lovely hair.* OCTAVIA *speaks excitedly.*] Siti, come here! Do you see the resemblance?

SITI. I have seen it from the first moment, my lady.

OCTAVIA. Strange that I could not.

SITI. Your eyes were blinded by tears.

OCTAVIA. Yes. [*Smiles down at* NUNA, *presses the jewel into her hand.*] Take this. It is yours.

NUNA. Mine!

OCTAVIA. To repay the debt I owe you.

NUNA. You mean it is really mine? I may do as I like with it?

OCTAVIA. You may do with it as you like.

NUNA. Then—I think I will give it to the baby as a birth-gift.

TIRZA. *Give* it! ⎤
⎥ [*Together.*]
GAIUS. It is worth a king's ransom! ⎦

BARSHAN. You can sell it for gold, girl!

LUCIUS. And buy your freedom.

OCTAVIA. [*Watching* NUNA *intently.*] Hush!

NUNA. [*Thinking it out.*] If I sold it—and bought my freedom—I would still have no mother and no home. I would still be lame. If I keep it—I shall always be frightened that someone will steal it from me. The baby will love it because it sparkles and is bright. It will give him pleasure. [*To* RACHEL.] May I take it in to him myself?

RACHEL. I will see. [*She goes through Center doors.*]

OCTAVIA. [*To* NUNA *who is starting up.*] Wait! I have a jacket of soft wool—it belonged to my little girl— [*Picks it up from among her things.*] I never thought to part with this—but take it.

LUCIUS. And take this. [*Holds out his cloak.*]

BARSHAN. You are giving away your great moment, soldier.

LUCIUS. [*A bit sheepishly.*] It is warm and a baby needs warmth.

TIRZA. I have a length of Egyptian cloth—very fine and well patterned. It will make him a little dress for the day he is carried to the temple.

BARSHAN. I will fetch it for you, and bring myrrh and incense to sweeten the air about him. [*Exits Right.*]

GAIUS. These wristlets are large for him now— [*Holds out the heavy metal wristlets he won earlier from* LUCIUS.] But he will grow into them.

[RACHEL *comes back, stands at Center doors.*]

SITI. [*Softly.*] I have nothing to give—except my love. Give him this.

[*Bends over and kisses* NUNA, *who smiles at them all, goes out.* RACHEL *holds one of the doors open for her to pass through, then closes it from the other side.*]

OCTAVIA. [*To* TIRZA.] The child Nuna is young and tender, unfit for heavy work. Will you sell her to me?

TIRZA. I will not sell her, my lady, no.

OCTAVIA. But I must have her. She is like my little daughter—the age she would have been now. I, who have never begged before—now beg you to let me have her to be a second daughter to me.

TIRZA. I did not say you could not have her—only that I would not sell. She is yours as a gift.

OCTAVIA. [*Taking* TIRZA's *hand.*] You are a good woman—and generous. [*The singing swells again.*] I seem to hear music.

TIRZA. I, too. [*Crosses to window, throws open the shutters. Light streams in.*] Look at the star!

GAIUS. How near it is!

OCTAVIA. And beautiful beyond words!

[BARSHAN *hurries in, carrying the Egyptian cloth and a small package of spices. He is followed by* AROD. BOTH *are so excited their speeches overlap.*]

BARSHAN. Mistress Tirza! Mistress Tirza! More guests!

AROD. The wise men we met in the North.

BARSHAN. With their soldiers and slaves.

AROD. They say the star has shown them the abode of the Prince of Peace—

BARSHAN. It is here!

GAIUS. Here! ⎤
OCTAVIA. Here? ⎦ [*Together.*]

AROD. They say he is a babe, new-born.

LUCIUS. There is no new-born Prince here.

OCTAVIA. Only a child of humble folk.

TIRZA. How should there be a Prince in my poor inn?

AROD. The shepherds say there is a sign by which they will know him.

BARSHAN. They will find him cradled in a manger.

OCTAVIA. A manger! ⎤
TIRZA. In a manger! ⎦ [*Together.*]

[ALL *turn their faces toward the double doors in awe and astonishment. They open and* NUNA *stands in the doorway, her face alight.*]

NUNA. I gave him the jewel. He reached out his little hand and— [*To* SITI.] I put your kiss upon it. Then he smiled and touched me—here. [*Touches her breast. The* ANGELS' MUSIC *swells again.*] Listen! The star is singing! [*Walks quickly, nimbly, across toward window.*]

OCTAVIA. Why, she can walk! ⎤
GAIUS. The girl is walking! ⎦ [*Together.*]

NUNA. [*Making the discovery with surprise.*] Yes! I am walking! I can walk! I can walk! [*In her joy and delight she throws her arms about* OCTAVIA.]

OCTAVIA. God bless you! [*Suddenly puzzled.*] Now why did I say "God" and not "the Gods"?

[*The* ANGELS' MUSIC *swells off Left and is joined by the* SHEPHERDS' CHORUS *which begins off Right. The door opens and the* WISE MEN *enter, followed in solemn procession by their slaves, the* SHEPHERDS, PILGRIMS *and* TOWNSPEOPLE. *At the first moment of entrance* RACHEL *and* LUCIUS *open the wide Center double-doors to disclose* MARY, *seated, with* JOSEPH *standing beside her. The red cloak is thrown across the back of the manger, reflecting light which is all that we see of the* HOLY INFANT.*
As the pageant of the Giving of Gifts proceeds, the music swells to a final triumphant chord. All movement ceases, turning the scene into a tableau of the Nativity.

CURTAIN

NEEDLEWORK

A Comedy in One Act

BY

FLORENCE RYERSON

CHARACTERS

MISS KEW

MRS. BROWN

GRAMMA PENNY

LILYMAE BUCKNER

MRS. STAPLES

MISS HARKNESS

MRS. WILLOBY

MR. WARDLE

GRACIA HALE

EFFIE McGILL

JUDY FLANNIGAN

SCENE

The Art Department of Carlson and Kew, Dry Goods and Notions, in Oakdale.

TIME

The present. Late on a winter afternoon.

NEEDLEWORK

The Curtain rises on a typical art department where materials for needlework are sold and lessons given in knitting, crocheting and other handicraft.

Along the Right wall are shelves containing boxes of wool with a counter upon which there is a telephone. Upper Right, curtains over a storage closet. Upper Center, the entrance from the main store. At Left, a large window looking down upon the street.

A low work table with chairs is down stage, a little to Left of Center. This is far enough away from the counter so that a conversation there cannot be heard at the table unless the voices are raised. Lower Left, a small table with two chairs. Upper Left, near the window, a table with pattern books and a chair. GRAMMA PENNY'S *rocker is midway between the tables with its back to the main entrance. Scattered about the room and hanging on the wall is a colorful display of handiwork, quilts, afghans, sweaters and hooked rugs with other oddments.*

At Rise: MISS KEW *stands behind the big table giving instructions to two pupils with professional sweetness. Seated at the table on her Left is* MRS. BROWN, *plump, grey-haired, not too bright. At her Right,* LILYMAE BUCKNER, *young and pretty.*

In a rocking chair, mid-stage, is GRAMMA PENNY, *as deaf as she is spry.* MISS HARKNESS, *grim and bony, sits above the small table, her back to the window. At her Left is* MRS.

WILLOBY *large, inclined to be pompous. She is working on a cross-stitched chair-seat.* MISS HARKNESS *is hooking a rug. All the* OTHERS *are knitting, including* MRS. STAPLES, *a sharp, bird-like little woman who seldom lights for long but flutters back and forth between the table and the window clicking her needles as she goes.*

All knitting needles are of steel, as is the spike MISS HARKNESS *uses on her rug and* MRS. WILLOBY'S *large yarn needle. There is something suggesting cruelty in the way they punctuate their conversation by stabbing their work with their sharp steel instruments.*

MISS KEW. [*Working on* MRS. BROWN'S *sweater.*] Twenty-two, twenty-three, twenty-four—six—eight—thirty, and knit two together for the gusset. There you are, dear. [*Returns knitting to* MRS. BROWN.] Just remember next time it's slip one, knit two together, slip two—no, I mean one, then knit one, I mean two, before you start the double purl. Perfectly simple.

MRS. BROWN. Not to me. I wish I'd stuck to mufflers.

MISS KEW. Oh, no, dear! We must keep making progress, mustn't we? Something a little more difficult every day.

GRAMMA PENNY. An apple a day keeps the doctor away.

MISS KEW. Goodness! You never know what Gramma's going to say, do you? Now Lilymae, what's your difficulty?

LILYMAE. Look at it! The darn thing's started whooshing up on me 'til I can't tell whether I'm knitting my sleeve or my waistline.

MRS. STAPLES. That's the trouble with those one-piecers. You never know where you are— [*Suddenly stares out window.*] Well, I declare!

[EVERYONE *tenses, ready to jump toward the window if it proves to be something interesting. This business is repeated throughout the play.*]

MISS HARKNESS. Who is it?

MRS. WILLOBY. What do you see? } [*Together.*]

MRS. STAPLES. That's the fourth time old man Carlson's come out of the Brass Rail Bar.

[*They* ALL *relax.*]

LILYMAE AND MRS. BROWN. Is that all!

GRAMMA PENNY. What'd she say?

MISS HARKNESS. She said old Carlson's come out of the Brass Rail four times.

GRAMMA PENNY. Is that all?

MRS. STAPLES. No, wait— [*They alert again.*] It is—no it isn't—yes, it *is*—Lucinda Braxton going into Modes and Manners!

MRS. WILLOBY. I heard she's getting a new hat.

MISS HARKNESS. She had a new hat last year.

MRS. BROWN. It was year before last.

MISS HARKNESS. Last year. It was brown with a green velvet bow and a buckle off her sister's old suit.

MRS. WILLOBY. That's right. Her year-before-last's was black. Why, hello, Professor.

[*This to* MR. WARDLE, *a gentle, near-sighted little man who sidles in obviously wishing himself elsewhere.*]

LILYMAE. Professor Wardle!

MRS. STAPLES. What are you doing here? } [*Together.*]

MISS HARKNESS. Planning to take up knitting, Professor?

MR. WARDLE. [*Unhappily, as he goes to counter.*] Good afternoon, Miss Kew, Mrs. Brown, Lilymae, Miss Harkness, Mrs.—er, Mrs.— [*Gives up. Speaks to* MISS KEW.] My wife, Mrs. Wardle, sent me—if you don't mind—

MISS KEW. [*Crossing to counter.*] Not at all.

MR. WARDLE. She's having trouble with her petitpoint. It's the wool. There doesn't seem to be enough of it. I've a sample— [*A fumbling search through his pockets which reveals a number of objects, including several bits of withered herbage.*] Botanical specimens. Oh, here it is. She wants two yards.

MISS KEW. I think you mean two *hanks,* Professor.

MR. WARDLE. Do I? Well—you're probably right.

MISS KEW. Now where did I put that petitpoint wool? Here? No. I'm sure I put it somewhere—

[*Begins rummaging around through shelves and boxes while* MR. WARDLE *waits nervously.*]

GRAMMA PENNY. Who's that at the counter?

MRS. BROWN. Just Professor Wardle.

LILYMAE. Professor Wardle from the High School.

GRAMMA PENNY. What's he want a high stool for?

MRS. WILLOBY. Not high stool. High School.

LILYMAE. He came for his wife.

GRAMMA PENNY. His wife here? I didn't see her.

MISS HARKNESS. No, no! He came to buy some yarn for his wife.

GRAMMA PENNY. Why couldn't you say so in the first place?

LILYMAE. I declare she gets more hard of hearing every day.

MISS KEW. [*Still rummaging.*] I could swear that wool was on this shelf only yesterday! Where it can have got to— [*Her voice dies away as she looks under counter.*]—I can't imagine.

MRS. STAPLES. [*Still at window looking down into street.*] Lucinda's coming out of Modes and Manners!

MRS. BROWN. New hat?

MRS. STAPLES. Yes! [*They ALL start to rise.*] No! [*They sit down again.*] It's her year-before-last's black with a new stick-up-'em on the side.

MISS KEW. [*Coming up with the wool.*] I think this is it. Let me see that sample. Why, Professor, your hand is shaking!

MR. WARDLE. I'm sorry. It's this place. It seems to affect me—

MISS KEW. Affect you?

MR. WARDLE. I—I think it's all the ladies sitting and knitting. Like the *tricoteuses*.

MISS KEW. The what?

MR. WARDLE. *Tricoteuses.* You know—all those bloody heads in the basket.

MISS KEW. Professor!

MR. WARDLE. From the guillotine. It's in *The Tale of Two Cities.*

MISS KEW. Oh, Charles Dickens!

MR. WARDLE. Everytime the women took a stitch another head fell in the basket.

MISS KEW. [*Kindly.*] I think you must mean every time they knitted a *row,* Professor.

MR. WARDLE. Perhaps you're right. Yes, undoubtedly—

MISS KEW. And the ladies aren't all knitting. Look at Miss Harkness— [MR. WARDLE *looks at* MISS HARKNESS, *who is savagely stabbing her rug with a stiletto-like instrument.*] She's hooking.

MR. WARDLE. [*With a little shudder.*] So I see.

MRS. STAPLES. [*Leaning toward window.*] She's gone into Schultz's Delicatessen.

MRS. BROWN. Who has?

MISS HARKNESS. Lucinda? } [*Together.*]

MRS. STAPLES. No. Gracia Hale.

MRS. WILLOBY. Probably going to give poor Jimmie cold cuts again.

MRS. STAPLES. No—it's not cold cuts— [*Leans forward,*

nose against the glass.] Schultz is putting something into a paper carton.

MISS HARKNESS. Potato salad.

MRS. STAPLES. [*Hot on the scent.*] Not potato salad either. Schultz is too far down the counter—

MRS. WILLOBY. Maybe it's pickled pigs' feet.

MRS. BROWN. I wouldn't put it past her!

MISS KEW. [*Handing over package.*] Here you are, Professor. And here's your slip. Come again.

MR. WARDLE. [*Absently.*] I hope not. That is, thank you. Thank you very much. Good afternoon, ladies. Goodbye—goodbye. [*He bumbles out to a chorus of* "Goodbye, Professor."]

LILYMAE. Can you picture yourself married to *that?*

MISS HARKNESS. She's just as bad as he is.

MRS. BROWN, MRS. WILLOBY, MISS KEW. [*Together.*] Worse!

MR. WARDLE. [*At door again.*] I beg your pardon— [*They* ALL *swing around guiltily.*]

MISS KEW. Oh, Professor!

MR. WARDLE. Where do you keep your corsets? I mean the store's corsets—the corset department.

MISS KEW. Corsets to the left.

MR. WARDLE. Thank you. My wife's broken her string.

[*They* ALL *remain frozen until he is gone.*]

MRS. WILLOBY. [*Breaking pose.*] Broken her string!

[*They* ALL *laugh;* MISS KEW *sits down by* LILYMAE.]

MISS KEW. Now let me see that knitting again, dear.

LILYMAE. What was he saying? The Professor?

MISS KEW. [*Busy with knitting.*] Nothing much. Two—four—six— Some crazy business about those women in Paris—knit two and purl one—*Tale of Two Cities*—

MRS. BROWN. [*To* LILYMAE.] What did she say he said?

LILYMAE. [*Over her shoulder.*] Something about the women in Paris. *Tale of Two Cities.*

MRS. WILLOBY. What's that about Paris dresses?

GRAMMA PENNY. They're making 'em with two tails.

MISS KEW. [*To* LILYMAE, *referring to sweater.*] You've got it back to front.

GRAMMA PENNY. [*To* MRS. WILLOBY.] Back to front.

MISS HARKNESS. I never! [*Calling up to* MRS. STAPLES.] Heard about the new Paris dresses? They're wearing 'em back to front!

MRS. STAPLES. I'm not surprised.

MISS HARKNESS. Me neither!

MISS KEW. [*Still busy with sweater.*] Two together six times and yarn over twelve times— Can you imagine? He said we reminded him of those French women—eight, ten, twelve—

LILYMAE. What French women?

MISS KEW. Those guillotine ones. He said every time they knitted a stitch, bang, went a head into the basket.

MRS. WILLOBY. What's she saying now?

GRAMMA PENNY. [*Who has been leaning over the arm of her rocker trying to hear, now leans over the other arm to convey the information.*] She says the French ladies knit a stitch every time the guillotine goes bang.

MISS HARKNESS. Up to their old tricks, h'm?

MRS. WILLOBY. Funny it isn't in the papers.

MISS HARKNESS. [*Darkly.*] Censorship. [*Calls to* MISS KEW.] Who told you that about the guillotine?

MISS KEW. Two, four, eight, Professor Wardle, ten, twelve.

MISS HARKNESS. Professor Wardle.

MRS. WILLOBY. Then it certainly must be true.

MISS HARKNESS. The French always were excitable.

MRS. WILLOBY. [*Nodding.*] Seems like they're never happy unless blood is running in their streets.

MRS. STAPLES. [*Calling from window.*] Who'd you say is running around the streets?

MRS. WILLOBY. She didn't say anyone was—

GRAMMA PENNY. Professor Wardle.

MRS. STAPLES. Why, he's nothing of the sort!

LILYMAE. [*Giggling.*] His wife wouldn't let him!

MRS. WILLOBY. And *that's* no lie!

GRAMMA PENNY. What's no lie?

MISS HARKNESS. That Mrs. Wardle won't let the Professor run around the streets.

MRS. BROWN. [*Surprised.*] Does he want to?

GRAMMA PENNY. At his age! The idea!

MRS. STAPLES. [*Suddenly.*] Pickles!

MRS. WILLOBY. Where?

MRS. BROWN. What did you say? } [*Together.*]

MRS. STAPLES. I just remembered what Schultz keeps in that jar at the end of the counter. Gracia Hale was buying dill pickles.

MISS HARKNESS. Well, that's better than pigs' feet.

GRAMMA PENNY. What's better than pigs' feet?

LILYMAE. Pickles, Gramma.

GRAMMA PENNY. [*Belligerently.*] Who says so?

MRS. BROWN. Nellie Harkness.

GRAMMA PENNY. I don't see why.

MRS. STAPLES. [*Leaning far over again to look out.*] She's coming into the store. Gracia Hale is.

MISS KEW. Probably after more nylons. Knit and over, knit and over.

GRAMMA PENNY. Pickles are pickles and pigs' feet are pigs' feet. You can't say one's better than the other.

MISS KEW. Jane Tolliver in hosiery says Gracia wears out two pairs of nylons every month of her life.

LILYMAE. That's what he gets for marrying her.

MRS. STAPLES. What who gets?

LILYMAE. Jimmie Hale. For marrying Gracia.

GRAMMA PENNY. Certainly they're married. I was at the wedding. I said then it'd never last.

MISS KEW. Well, you've got to admit it's lasted four years.

MISS HARKNESS. Three.

MISS KEW. Four. Junior takes a three-year pattern.

GRAMMA PENNY. I still don't see what that's got to do with pickles.

GRACIA. [*From door.*] Who said "pickles"? That's a coincidence! I've got some right here! [*Enters waving a paper carton. She is a pleasantly pretty young person, simply dressed but in good style. Possesses a nice smile and a dry sense of humor. The group greets her with a chorus of* "Hello, Gracia!" "How are you, Gracia?" *etc. ad lib.*] I'm fine. But in a hurry. Jimmie flew to New York last night—

MISS HARKNESS. No!

MRS. STAPLES. To New York? } [*Together.*]

GRACIA. Don't tell me the Gestapo failed to report it! [*To* MISS KEW *who has moved to counter.*] I'd like some white wool, please. Two ply.

MISS KEW. White wool, two ply. I used to keep it right here but there isn't much demand for two ply so— Now where do you suppose I moved it?

[*Business of searching through shelves and boxes again while* GRACIA *turns away from counter.*]

GRACIA. That's good-looking, Lilymae. What is it? No, don't tell me! It's a net for catching fish!

LILYMAE. It's my new evening sweater.

GRACIA. Well, you'll have to admit I came close.

MRS. STAPLES. [*Again at window.*] Effie McGill's back home from Kansas City! She's got a new fur piece!

[MRS. BROWN *and* MISS HARKNESS *drop their work and hurry up to window.*]

MRS. BROWN. That's right!

MISS HARKNESS. Silver fox!

LILYMAE. Bet it's just one of her Aunt's old collars done over.

MISS HARKNESS. Could be—

GRACIA. Sorry to disappoint you. She bought it in Kansas City—Jellifee's fur department.

MRS. STAPLES. Jellifee's?

GRACIA. Yes. I happened to run into her while she was there. [*Goes back to counter, speaking impishly over her shoulder.*] Now all you've got to do is figure out how she paid for it.

MRS. BROWN. [*Quite without humor.*] I wonder, how did she?

LILYMAE. [*Crossing to window.*] I know for a fact that the library only pays her twenty-five a week.

MISS HARKNESS. And it costs her fifteen for room and board.

[*They stand figuring it up on their fingers as* MISS KEW *comes back to* GRACIA.]

MISS KEW. I found where I'd put it—but we're out of it.

GRACIA. Oh, dear! I've got to turn out a layette in a hurry. I ought to have started long ago but you know how it is—I kept putting it off until now it's a race between me and the stork— [*Catches* MISS KEW's *interested stare.*] Nugh-ugh! He's bringing his little bundle to my sister-in-law.

MISS KEW. I didn't know you had a sister-in-law.

GRACIA. Jimmie's brother's wife. They've just moved to Kansas City from New York so I feel I've got to watch out for them.

MRS. BROWN. [*In group by window.*] Effie's Uncle Tom sometimes gives her a check for Christmas.

MISS HARKNESS. But he's in Europe.

MRS. WILLOBY. And this isn't Christmas.

MRS. BROWN. That's right.

MISS KEW. [*Getting out wool box at counter.*] Maybe you could use Iceland wool but we only have pink and blue.

GRACIA. That's lovely and soft. I'll take the pink. My sister-in-law's hoping for a little girl.

MISS KEW. I always say girls are nicest. So gentle and sweet.

LILYMAE. [*Shrilly.*] Well, you'll never convince *me* she paid for it herself!

MISS HARKNESS. Me, neither!

MRS. STAPLES. Not out of twenty-five a week!

GRACIA. [*Selecting wool.*] Bill, that's my husband's brother, doesn't care which it is, boy or girl— [*Indicating wool.*] This will do. Six hanks. He's so tickled he's just about out of his mind. Keeps on sending her flowers and bringing her presents.

MISS KEW. Some men are like that— [*Putting wool in envelope.*] And then again, some aren't.

MRS. STAPLES. [*Leaning against window again.*] Effie's coming into the store. Maybe she'll come up.

GRACIA. [*Moving Left.*] Goodie! Goodie! Then you can ask her about that neckpiece. Did she come by it honestly or— [*To* MRS. WILLOBY *who is holding a minute knitted sun-suit up against her ample bosom to flatten it out for measuring.*] That's pretty, Mrs. Willoby, but isn't it a trifle small?

MRS. WILLOBY. It's not for me. It's for my niece.

GRAMMA PENNY. What some girls will wear!

MRS. WILLOBY. [*Coldly.*] She is only three.

MISS KEW. [*Bringing wool to* GRACIA.] Here you are, dear.

GRACIA. Thank you. I've got to hurry. I've left Junior with Mrs. Flannigan and she wants to go home as soon as she finishes the ironing.

MRS. STAPLES. [*Coming over to counter.*] That looked like baby wool you were buying.

GRACIA. It was—and is. [*Moving toward door.*] I won't spoil your sport by telling you whose baby's going to wear it. [*From door.*] You can have the fun of figuring it out for yourselves. 'Bye! [*She is off.*]

MRS. BROWN. Well, what d'you think of that?

MRS. WILLOBY. *I* call it impudence!

LILYMAE. Thinks she's so smart just because she's from New York.

MISS HARKNESS. [*Stabbing her rug viciously.*] And an actress.

MISS KEW. Only on television, dear.

MRS. BROWN. That's just as bad.

LILYMAE AND MISS HARKNESS. Worse!

MRS. WILLOBY. I came very near going on the stage once. I took elocution lessons for years. [*Unconsciously using her chest tones and best Delsarte gesture.*] Pray pass the shears.

MISS KEW. [*Handing over a pair from table.*] I've got to run down to the stock room. If anyone comes, tell 'em I'll be right back.

MRS. STAPLES. [*Calling, as* MISS KEW *goes out.*] Wait a minute! Who was Gracia buying that wool for?

MISS KEW. [*Her voice dying away as she goes off.*] She *said* it was for her sister—

GRAMMA PENNY. Who was she talking about?

LILYMAE. Gracia's sister.

GRAMMA PENNY. Gracia hasn't got a sister.

MRS. BROWN. That's right. She hasn't.

LILYMAE. I remember. She told me she was an only child.

MRS. WILLOBY. She told me that, too.

MRS. STAPLES. You ask me—*she's* the one that's going to have it.

MISS HARKNESS. You took the words right out of my mouth.

GRAMMA PENNY. What's she take out of your mouth?

LILYMAE. We're talking about Gracia's baby.

GRAMMA PENNY. Navy! Why's she going to join the navy?

LILYMAE. Not navy, Gramma. *Baby.*

[EFFIE McGILL *enters. Plump; in her thirties; wears a small silver fox neckpiece and carries a knitting bag.*]

MRS. WILLOBY. [*Broadcasting to* GRAMMA *very distinctly.*] Gracia Hale's going to have a baby.

EFFIE. [*Coming down.*] Is she really?

[EVERYONE *looks beautifully surprised.*]

MRS. BROWN. Effie!

MISS HARKNESS. Why, it's Effie McGill! } [*Together.*]

LILYMAE. When did you get back?

MRS. STAPLES. [*Comes down from window, staring at the neckpiece. All other eyes are on it, too.*] We thought you were planning to stay a week.

EFFIE. I was. But I decided I'd rather spend my money on a fur than on hotel bills, so I bought this—and came home.

MRS. BROWN. [*Flatly.*] Oh, so *that's* how—

MISS HARKNESS. Very sensible of you, dear.

GRAMMA PENNY. [*Sotto voce to* MRS. WILLOBY *as* EFFIE *proudly shakes out the fur.*] Skimpy!

LILYMAE. [*A trifle catty.*] Mm. I think those single skins are so much more becoming than the double—don't you?

MISS HARKNESS. Especially when you're putting on a mite of weight.

EFFIE. Do you know, that's what I thought when I saw Gracia in the city. [*Sits down, takes out knitting.*] I said to myself, "I do believe she's putting on weight." But I never thought it might be—did she tell you about it?

MRS. STAPLES. No, but she was just in buying baby wool.

LILYMAE. [*Giggling.*] She pretended it was for somebody else.

EFFIE. Why?

MRS. WILLOBY. That's what I'd like to know.

MRS. STAPLES. You'd think she might have told us in confidence.

MRS. BROWN. Secretive—that's what she is! [*Having trouble with her knitting.*] Gracious, this is loose!

GRAMMA PENNY. [*Severely.*] I wouldn't say that.

MRS. BROWN. Say what?

GRAMMA PENNY. Gracia may be flighty, but she isn't loose.

MRS. BROWN. I didn't say "Gracia" I said "Gracious."

GRAMMA PENNY. I heard very well what you said.

MRS. STAPLES. [*At that window again.*] What's that about Gracia?

LILYMAE. Gramma thought Mrs. Brown said Gracia was loose.

MRS. STAPLES. I've always thought so myself. Mind you, I wouldn't have been the *first* to say it—

MRS. BROWN. But I *didn't* say it!

MRS. STAPLES. [*Not listening.*] What I contend is—she laughs too much.

MRS. BROWN. I had a cousin like that. Laughing, laughing, all day long.

MRS. WILLOBY. What happened to her?

MRS. BROWN. [*Surprised.*] Why, nothing.

GRAMMA PENNY. [*Turning around in her chair.*] *What* happened?

LILYMAE. Nothing, Gramma.

GRAMMA PENNY. Then why bring her up? [*Breaks off as* JUDY FLANNIGAN, *a girl of ten or twelve, hurries in breathlessly.*] Isn't that Mrs. Flannigan's Judy?

MRS. BROWN. Why, yes. Do you want something, Judy?

JUDY. No, ma'am. But Mrs. Hale does. [*Stops an instant to catch her breath. They* ALL *focus on her.*] She wants to change this pink wool for blue on account of the baby's got a fifty-fifty chance of having red hair.

MRS. BROWN. Red hair!

MISS HARKNESS. What's that? } [*Together.*]

LILYMAE. Not really!

JUDY. Yes, ma'am. Mrs. Hale'd forgotten about the hair when she bought pink. So now she wants blue.

MRS. STAPLES. [*Excitedly.*] I know where the wool is—I'll get it for you. [*Moves upstage with* JUDY *following.*]

MRS. BROWN. [*As soon as* JUDY *is out of earshot.*] Jimmie hasn't red hair.

MRS. WILLOBY. I should say he hasn't!

LILYMAE. It's black as black!

EFFIE. [*A sudden gasp.*] Oh!

MISS HARKNESS. What's the matter!

EFFIE. [*Indicating* JUDY.] Sh!

LILYMAE. Tell us! Tell us!

GRAMMA PENNY. [*As they lean closer.*] You look fit to burst!

EFFIE. *He* had red hair!

MRS. WILLOBY. He?

MISS HARKNESS. Who?

EFFIE. The man she was with in the city!

LILYMAE. Gracia was with?

GRAMMA PENNY. Talk louder. I can't hear you.

EFFIE. It was red as fire.

LILYMAE, MISS HARKNESS, MRS. WILLOBY. [*Rapidly, one after the other.*]
Who was he?
Where'd you see them?
What were they doing?

EFFIE. [*Trying to answer all three at once.*] I don't know who. In Jellifee's fur department. Buying a fur coat.

MRS. WILLOBY. [*In delight.*] A fur coat!

EFFIE. Mink. Down to *here*.

MRS. BROWN. Why didn't you *tell* us?

EFFIE. I haven't had time.

GRAMMA PENNY. Tell us what? I want to know.

MRS. BROWN. Somebody bought Gracia a mink coat.

GRAMMA PENNY. It won't set well. Pink's not her color.

LILYMAE. Not *pink*, Gramma. Mink.

EFFIE. Down to here!

MRS. STAPLES. [*Rushing* JUDY *toward door in order to get back into the discussion.*] There you are, Judy. Now you hurry right back. It's getting late.

JUDY. Yes'm, I know and Mrs. Hale's got to pack. [*Starts off on the run.*]

MRS. STAPLES. Judy! Wait! [*Goes after her, brings her back, wriggling and protesting.*]

JUDY. I can't wait! Mrs. Hale's in a terrible hurry.

MISS HARKNESS. In a hurry?

MRS. STAPLES. Why?   } [*Together.*]

EFFIE. Did you say she's packing?

LILYMAE. Packing to go where?

JUDY. To Kansas City. She's got to get off right away quick, and Mama's going to take care of Junior.

MRS. STAPLES. Why's she leaving so suddenly?

LILYMAE. She didn't say anything about it when she was here.

JUDY. He only just phoned her. [*Breaks away, starts for the door.*] She's got to catch the next train 'cause he's meeting her in the city. 'Bye!

MRS. BROWN. Who telephoned?

MRS. WILLOBY. Where'd you say he's meeting her? } [*Together.*]

MRS. STAPLES. Wait a minute! Judy! Come back here! [*Realizes she has gone, hurries out after her.*]

EFFIE. Well, I must say!

MISS HARKNESS. What do you think of that?

MRS. BROWN. Words fail me!

MRS. WILLOBY. Leaving little Junior! That's what I can't get over!

EFFIE. Me, too!

MRS. BROWN. Poor Junior!

GRAMMA PENNY. Poor Junior? What's the matter with Junior?

LILYMAE. Nothing, Gramma.

MRS. BROWN. Gracia's leaving him with Mrs. Flannigan.

GRAMMA PENNY. Then I say, "poor Flannigan"! If there ever was a young hellion—

MRS. STAPLES. [*Panting back in.*] Got away before I could catch her.

GRAMMA PENNY. Lying on the floor, kicking and screaming—

MRS. STAPLES. [*Comes down, hurriedly.*] You still talking about Gracia?

LILYMAE. Yes.

MRS. STAPLES. Well, I've heard a lot about her, but I must say I've never heard *that!*

EFFIE. What?

MRS. STAPLES. About her lying on the floor and—

MRS. WILLOBY. [*Cutting in.*] Gramma didn't say Gracia—

EFFIE. Gramma said Junior.

GRAMMA PENNY. What you sayin' about me?

MISS HARKNESS. Nothing about you, Gramma.

EFFIE. I was just explaining what you said about the kicking and screaming—

GRAMMA PENNY. It's the truth. Heard it with my own ears!

[MISS KEW *comes back in carrying boxes.*]

MISS KEW. I got caught by Mrs. Tolliver and you know how she gossips! All about that daughter of hers who's gone to Reno.

GRAMMA PENNY. Who's gone to Reno?

[*They ignore her, each anxious to be the first to give the great news.*]

MRS. BROWN. Never mind about Mrs. Tolliver—

EFFIE. Wait until we tell you—

MISS HARKNESS. Have you heard about Gracia?

MRS. STAPLES. Gracia and Jimmie?

GRAMMA PENNY. [*Catching hold of* LILYMAE.] Has Jimmie gone to Reno?

LILYMAE. [*A quick aside.*] Mrs. Tolliver's daughter, Gramma.

GRAMMA PENNY. Great Day!

MISS KEW. I haven't heard anything.

LILYMAE. Gracia's leaving Jimmie!

MRS. STAPLES. She's running away.

MRS. WILLOBY. With a man from Kansas City.

EFFIE. With red hair.

MISS KEW. Why, I can't believe it! She was only just *in* here! Are you sure?

MISS HARKNESS. [*Indignantly.*] Would we say so if we weren't?

LILYMAE. He's been buying her fur coats.

EFFIE. [*Trying to be accurate.*] It was only *one* coat.

MRS. STAPLES. You mean you only *saw* one.

MRS. WILLOBY. Anyway, it was mink.

MISS HARKNESS, LILYMAE, EFFIE. [*Together.*] Down to here!

MISS KEW. [*Sinks on chair.*] Well, I declare! And her only just buying baby wool—calm as calm!

MISS HARKNESS. You never know, do you?

GRAMMA PENNY. [*Rising and going to them.*] You never know what? What're you sayin' now?

LILYMAE. It's still about Gracia, Gramma.

MRS. STAPLES. She and Jimmie are splitting up.

MRS. BROWN. She's leaving him.

GRAMMA PENNY. Didn't I say it wouldn't last?

MRS. BROWN. [*To* OTHERS; *much impressed.*] That's right! She did!

GRAMMA PENNY. So that's why Jimmie went to Reno!

MRS. WILLOBY. Has Jimmie gone to Reno?

MISS HARKNESS. I thought he was in New York.

MRS. STAPLES. We only have Gracia's word for it.

MISS KEW. That's right. [*To* GRAMMA.] Where'd you hear about his being in Reno?

GRAMMA PENNY. [*Rolling her eyes.*] I get around!

MR. WARDLE. [*Re-entering in his hesitant fashion.*] Good afternoon, ladies. Er—good afternoon again.

MISS KEW. Why, Professor!

MRS. STAPLES. You back? } [*Together.*]

MR. WARDLE. Er—yes. Yes, I am. [*To* MISS KEW.] My wife's broken her hoops.

GRAMMA PENNY. Whoops?

MR. WARDLE. Those round things she uses to hold her petit-point. [*To* MISS KEW.] She said you'd know the size.

MISS KEW. [*Distractedly.*] Hoops, hoops—now let me see— [*Starts pawing over the shelves again.*]—hoops.

[*Not interested, the* WOMEN *move Left with the exception of* GRAMMA, *who remains with* MR. WARDLE *at the counter.*]

LILYMAE. Almost four-thirty! My goodness! I certainly must be starting along home!

MRS. STAPLES. Me, too!

MISS HARKNESS. I'll go with you—soon as I clear this needle.

GRAMMA PENNY. [*Giggling to* MR. WARDLE.] They can't wait to spread the news about Gracia and Jimmie.

MR. WARDLE. Gracia and—you don't mean the Hales?

GRAMMA PENNY. Don't tell me you haven't heard!

MR. WARDLE. [*Anxiously.*] Nothing's happened to them?

GRAMMA PENNY. [*Leans toward him, speaks in a mysterious voice.*] They've fiffed.

MR. WARDLE. What?

GRAMMA PENNY. Fiffed. Split up.

MR. WARDLE. But surely not! Why, they live right across the street. I saw her only a few minutes ago.

GRAMMA PENNY. So did we, but she's leaving tonight. He's already gone to Reno.

MR. WARDLE. Dear, dear!

GRAMMA PENNY. [*Still more confidentially.*] With Mrs. Tolliver's daughter.

MR. WARDLE. That *is* bad! They've always seemed so happy.

GRAMMA PENNY. You can't really blame Jimmie. Gracia's been runnin' around loose. Chasin' to the city—buyin' mink coats—down to here.

LILYMAE. [*Who has moved in from Left.*] If you ask me, he's well rid of her.

MRS. STAPLES. [*Joining them.*] That's what I say! A grown woman throwing herself on the floor, kicking and screaming!

MISS KEW. [*Stopping her search.*] Does she really?

MRS. STAPLES. What everybody says!

GRAMMA PENNY. [*Wagging her head.*] Plain to see where Junior got it from!

MR. WARDLE. But really—living right across the street—it seems strange I haven't heard her!

MRS. STAPLES. [*Coldly.*] *Very* strange.

MISS KEW. I had a neighbor like that once—only with him it was drink. He'd roll home drunk every week-end—still does, I hear.

GRAMMA PENNY. He does!

MISS KEW. Mm. Smashes all the furniture and the windows. [*To* MR. WARDLE.] I can't seem to find your size. I'll look in the stock room.

[*Trots out as* GRAMMA *scuttles across room to the* OTHERS *who are gathering up their work and putting on coats and hats.*]

GRAMMA PENNY. Hear what Miss Kew says about Jimmie

Hale? Rolling home drunk every week-end. Smashing up all their furniture!

MRS. WILLOBY. What?
EFFIE. Honestly? } [*Together.*]

GRAMMA PENNY. She's heard him herself.

MRS. WILLOBY. She does live quite close—

EFFIE. Just over the back fence.

MISS HARKNESS. I remember they had a chair fixed last week. Gracia said Junior broke the leg.

GRAMMA PENNY. He broke Junior's leg!

MISS HARKNESS. No! Junior broke the leg—chasing his dog. At least that's what *Gracia* said.

GRAMMA PENNY. [*Back to the counter.*] Did you hear about Jimmie's chasing Junior's dog and breaking its leg?

MR. WARDLE. I don't believe it! He would never do that!

MRS. STAPLES. You never can tell what a man'll do when he's drunk!

MR. WARDLE. But he doesn't drink. If he did I'd be sure to know!

MRS. STAPLES. You didn't know about Gracia's rolling around on the floor—

GRAMMA PENNY. —Kicking and screaming.

MR. WARDLE. No, but—

MRS. STAPLES. So you see!

MISS KEW. [*Comes back in, waving embroidery hoops.*] Hoops!

MR. WARDLE. Pardon? Oh, thank you. Thank you.

[*The telephone rings.*]

MISS KEW. [*Answering.*] Hello—yes, this is Needlework—no, Mrs. Hale isn't here.

GRAMMA PENNY. For Gracia?

MISS KEW. New York's calling her. [*Into telephone.*] Yes, if she comes I'll have her call you.

MRS. WILLOBY. Who was that?

MISS HARKNESS. Why'd they call her here?

[*Together, as she hangs up.*]

MISS KEW. Operator Eight. She called the house and they said Gracia was on her way down here.

LILYMAE. Down here! Well! [*Sits down; takes out her knitting again.*]

MRS. STAPLES. I thought you were in such a hurry, dear!

LILYMAE. Think I'm going to miss it?

MR. WARDLE. [*Nervously, as all the* OTHERS *get out their knitting again.*] You needn't trouble to wrap those, Miss Kew.

MISS KEW. [*Who has forgotten about the hoops.*] Oh, no trouble—no trouble at all— [*She breaks off as he takes the hoops out of her hand and starts a hurried escape.*] Mr. Wardle! You haven't your charge slip!

MR. WARDLE. [*Intent upon getting away.*] It's all right. You can slip it to me later.

[*He runs head on into* GRACIA *who is entering.*]

GRACIA. Why, hello, Professor! This *is* luck! [*Tucks her arm into his.*] I saw your car outside. If you'll wait one little minute I'll let you drive me home.

MR. WARDLE. [*Flustered.*] Excuse me. I mean, thank you. I mean, I'll be delighted.

GRACIA. Why, Professor, you're white as a sheet! You're actually shaking! Have the girls been scaring you? [*To* OTHERS.] Why don't you pick on someone your size? Me, for instance? [*Returns wool bag to* MISS KEW.] You gave Judy the wrong wool. Three ply instead of two. [*Discovers they are* ALL *staring at her.*] What's the matter? My petticoat showing? I ran out in a hurry. I've put in a phone call to New York and I want to get back before it comes through.

MISS KEW. It's already come.

MISS HARKNESS. They called here.

GRACIA. Good!

MRS. STAPLES. You're to ask for Operator—

MRS. WILLOBY. Number Eight.

MR. WARDLE. [*Unhappily, as all the* WOMEN *cluster around.*] It might be better to wait until you reach home.

GRACIA. No, sir! I've got a surprise for Jimmie and— [*Into telephone.*] Number Eight, please— [*To the* OTHERS.] I want to catch him before he gets away— [*Into telephone.*] Number Eight? This is Mrs. Hale—that New York call. Fine! [*To* MISS KEW, *who is changing the wool while the* OTHERS *cluster around* GRACIA.] He's flying home tomorrow, and he's going to find me missing. [*Into telephone.*] Yes, I'm waiting. [*To* MISS KEW *again.*] My sister-in-law's baby's coming sooner than we expected.

GRAMMA PENNY. Who'd she say was coming?

[*They* ALL *shush her.*]

GRACIA. [*Into telephone; her voice full of affection.*] Hello! That you, Jimmie? You okay? Me, too, darling. Terribly— but I've got to catch the train to Kansas City. You guessed it! Red's nearly frantic—Mm—I've got to go up and hold his hand. [*The* WOMEN *gradually droop in disappointment.*] And listen, angel, he wants you to do him a favor— Mm—look over a few fur coats—mink—

EFFIE. [*Enlightened.*] Oh!

GRACIA. Red got her one for a having-a-baby present but he's decided it isn't good enough—he wants one from New York. You might bring me one, too. [*Listens, giggles.*] Don't be silly! [*Realizes she has an audience.*] I can't talk now. Tell you what—I'll be home in ten minutes. Call me there. I promised Junior he could speak to his Daddy— Okay! 'Bye, love! [*Hangs up, puts her hand on* MR. WAR-DLE'S *arm.*] Want to beau me home?

MR. WARDLE. [*Expansively.*] Delighted! De-lighted! If you ladies will excuse us— [*Pushes his way through the group, going toward exit.*]

GRACIA. [*Stops suddenly.*] My wool! I was forgetting! [*Runs back, takes bag from* MISS KEW, *hurries back to re-join* MR. WARDLE, *waving bag as she goes.*] Happy knitting!

MRS. STAPLE, MISS HARKNESS, MRS. BROWN. [*As* GRACIA *exits with* MR. WARDLE.] *Well!*

GRAMMA PENNY. [*Bewildered; looking from the door to group.*] What I want to know—who said they were splitting up?

EVERYONE. [*At once.*]
Why, *she* did!
She did!
She did!
You did!

They are ALL *pointing knitting needles at each other accusingly as*

THE CURTAIN FALLS

DOUBLE DATE

A Comedy in One Act

BY

FLORENCE RYERSON

CHARACTERS

MRS. LILLIAN BARTON
TUCKER BARTON
UNCLE CLAIBOURNE TUCKER
BABS PRINGLE
GILBERT PRINGLE
GEORGIA BARTON
MARYLEE MORSE

SCENE

Living-room of Mrs. Barton's house in Irvington.

TIME

The present. Morning of a Spring day.

NOTE

The speech of all the characters in this play, especially that of Mrs. Barton, should suggest the South, but the players must be careful not to over-emphasize their accents.

DOUBLE DATE

The living-room of the Barton house is pleasantly bright, if a little old-fashioned. The set is raked so that the entrance hall is visible at Right with the lower steps and landing of the stairs. At Left, a door into the dining-room. Upper Center, French windows with a glimpse of garden.

Furniture, comfortable with, perhaps, a suggestion of Southern Victorian. A divan, several easy chairs, a table with telephone. On the wall, upper Left, a mirror.

At Rise: MRS. BARTON *is entering from the dining-room. She is a plumply pretty little woman, scatter-brained in a charming Southern fashion. She wears a small apron over her morning dress, carries a cup of coffee and a piece of toast. In speaking she drops an occasional g, but not all of them.*

MRS. BARTON. [*Starting speech before Curtain rises.*] — With all I've got to do this mornin' I haven't time for breakfast. First thing, I must call Mr. Twillinger. [*By now the Curtain is up and she has reached the telephone. She does a juggling act with her cup and toast, nibbling and sipping while she dials and talks.*]—9—3—9—Good mornin'— Southern Costume Company?—May I speak to Mr. Twillinger?—Oh, Mr. Twillinger, is that you? This is Mrs. Ba'ton—*Barton*—just one little minute 'til I swallow this toast— [*Gets rid of mouthful, also cup.*] There now! Mr. Twillinger, do you recollect that Carnival costume my daughter Georgie picked out before she went back to boardin' school? The one she wanted—and then she didn't want it— and now she wants it again? It's red—with a hoop-skirt and ruffles—no, the ruffles don't go 'round and 'round—they scallop up and down—up and down—like this—

[*She is demonstrating how they scallop as* TUCKER BARTON, *sixteen, very sure about everything, enters from dining-room. He is eating two sugared doughnuts, holding one in either hand.*]

TUCKER. He can't see you, Mom.

MRS. BARTON. [*Into telephone.*] That's right! Scarlet O'Hara! Look out! You're crumbling! Not you, Mr. Twillinger! I was speaking to Tucker. He's eating doughnuts all over the floor.

TUCKER. You make me sound like I was two years old!

MRS. BARTON. You still have it? Thank goodness! And will you please pick out a costume for Gilbert Pringle to match? He and Georgia are goin' together—oh, he was? [*To* TUCKER, *with a little giggle.*] He says Gil was there waitin' when he opened up this mornin'.

TUCKER. The dope!

MRS. BARTON. Tucker, you hush! [*To* UNCLE CLAIBOURNE TUCKER, *a fat and grizzled oldster with a humorous expression who has just entered from dining-room.*] And you hush, too!

UNCLE CLAIBOURNE. Did I say anything?

MRS. BARTON. You were goin' to. [*Into telephone.*] We're expectin' Georgie home on the two o'clock. I'll send her down— No, Tucker doesn't need a costume. He's still right stubborn about not attendin'— Yes, I'll tell him you said so. [*Hangs up.*] Mr. Twillinger says every man-soul in town's going to be there t'night.

TUCKER. Uncle Claibourne isn't.

UNCLE CLAIBOURNE. Got too much sense. I'm goin' fishin'.

TUCKER. See, Mom?

MRS. BARTON. I do wish you'd stop encouragin' him, Uncle Clay. [*To* TUCKER.] With your best friend takin' Georgie looks to me like you'd want to invite some other girl and have a good—

TUCKER. [*Interrupting on cue "girl."*] Just because I see Gil walking into a buzz-saw's no reason for me to do the same.

MRS. BARTON. [*Interrupting on cue "reason."*] Tucker Barton! It isn't nice-folks to call your sister a buzz-saw!

TUCKER. I didn't, Mom!

UNCLE CLAIBOURNE. [*Looking around.*] What low-down lack-wit's mislaid my dry-flies?

MRS. BARTON. You put 'em in that table drawer. [*To* TUCKER *again.*] Hear you talk, anybody'd think you didn't love your sister a-tall!

TUCKER. She's all right as a sister, but as a gal-pal for Gil she's strictly nugh-ugh.

MRS. BARTON. [*Indignantly.*] Like to know why!

TUCKER. Well—I'm not sayin' she's a park-n'-kisser, but she's sure a date-digger and brusher-offer, isn't she Uncle Clay?

UNCLE CLAIBOURNE. [*Rummaging in drawer.*] She'd snatch your tail-feathers an' use 'em for a fan.

MRS. BARTON. Uncle Claibourne!

TUCKER. Well, she would, Mom! Georgie'll say yeah-yeah to any prospect wants to date her, but let a bigger an' better give her the howl—she'll whoosh off without sayin' bye-bye!

MRS. BARTON. I declare, you're the no-manner'dest brother I ever *did* see! [*Turns on* UNCLE CLAIBOURNE.] And you're to blame! How d'you expect him to keep his ideals of womanhood?

UNCLE CLAIBOURNE. That's a fair question. Son, if you want to hang onto your ideals of womanhood, you jus' keep away from girls and come fishin' with me.

MRS. BARTON. Oh!

TUCKER. You betcha! Quick as I get my boots 'n tackle! }[*Together.*]

[BABS PRINGLE, *about twelve, in blue jeans and a bedraggled T-shirt appears at French windows.*]

BABS. Can I go with you, Tucker?

TUCKER. No, you can't!

MRS. BARTON. Babs! What were you doing there?

TUCKER. What's she always doin'?

BABS. I wasn't either! I just happened to overhear because I didn't want to bother you by ringing the front door-bell. [*To* MRS. BARTON.] Mama's kind thanks and here's the pattern she borrowed for Gil's sweater and I met a messenger boy coming up the walk. I guess he must've thought I lived here—

TUCKER. He was right.

BABS. —because he gave me this special delivery letter.

MRS. BARTON. [*Taking letter.*] From Georgie! Now what do you suppose—

BABS. Bet she's changed her mind again 'bout going to the Carnival with Gil.

TUCKER. She better hadn't!

BABS. I should say not! Dad says he never *did* see Gil so chuckle-headed over anything as he's chuckle-headed over Georgie an' that damn' Carnival—

MRS. BARTON. Babs!

BABS. Well, that's what Dad calls it. He says the only duff'rence between Gil and our bull-calf is the calf's got some sense.

MRS. BARTON. [*Vaguely, as she reads letter.*] I'm sure Georgie wouldn't do anything to hurt Gil—oh, dear!

BABS. What's the matter?

UNCLE CLAIBOURNE. Want I should take Tucker out before his faith in womanhood gets destroyed some more?

MRS. BARTON. [*Still reading.*] Yes— [*Realizes what she is saying.*] Oh, you hush! [*Crosses to phone, looking worried. Dials.*]—9—3—9—Southern Costume? Is that you, Mr. Twillinger? This is Mrs. Barton—

UNCLE CLAIBOURNE. Mother of Lucretia Georgia Barton.

MRS. BARTON. [*Ignoring him.*] —I'm so sorry to trouble you again, but there's been a little misunderstanding about dates—

TUCKER. Huh!

UNCLE CLAIBOURNE. Ha! } [*Together.*]

[BABS *merely giggles.*]

MRS. BARTON. It seems Georgie'd completely forgotten this was the week-end she was going to the V.M.I. hop with her roommate's brother—

TUCKER. Because he'd completely forgotten to invite her.

MRS. BARTON. [*Still into telephone, giving him a look.*] No, I don't know about Gil's costume. I'll ask him to call you if he happens to drop in. [*Hurriedly, one eye on TUCKER who is pounding a sofa pillow in his wrath.*] Thank you for bein' so understandin'. Goodbye. [*As she hangs up.*] Now, Tucker, honey, you mustn't blame Georgie—

TUCKER. Not blame her!

UNCLE CLAIBOURNE. [*Tongue in cheek.*] It's a lady's privilege to change her beau.

MRS. BARTON. [*Taking him seriously.*] Of course. Stands to reason Georgie'd never have accepted for the Carnival if she'd known she was going to be invited to V.M.I.

UNCLE CLAIBOURNE. But she'd pure given up hope.

MRS. BARTON. Absolutely. 'Course the Carnival's just a home-town ball and Gil's just a home-town boy, while a V.M.I. bid's mighty hard to come by.

UNCLE CLAIBOURNE. A girl's got to look out for herself.

MRS. BARTON. Mm. How else is she going to be popular? [*Suddenly realizes she is being kidded.*] Oh, go'long!

TUCKER. But what about *Gil?* Gosh! You don't know what it's going to do to him! He can't just toss girls off the way I can. He doesn't understand anything *about* them.

MRS. BARTON. Then it's high time he learned. Isn't it, Uncle Clay?

UNCLE CLAIBOURNE: Mm—yes. The female of the species isn't what you'd call a rarity. He'd be certain-sure to run into her sometime as she steamed along—

MRS. BARTON. [*To* TUCKER.] So you'd better hurry over and break it to him gently. Tell him Georgie sends a message. [*Looks through letter.*] She says she couldn't be sorrier but she knows he'll understand 'cause he's such a sweet little ole sugar-lump.

TUCKER. [*Flopping face-down over the back of a chair.*] Oh, nausea!

BABS. There comes Gil now. Over the back fence.

MRS. BARTON. Good! [*To* TUCKER.] That'll give you a chance to tell him.

TUCKER. [*Rising in wrath.*] I'll tell him all right! I'll tell him exactly the kind of a two-timing *reptile* little Georgie-pie *is!*

MRS. BARTON. [*As she moves Left.*] Oh, no, you won't! [*To* BABS.] Come on, honey. [*To* TUCKER *again.*] You won't say a word about your sister that isn't sweet an' kind.

TUCKER. [*Fiercely.*] I'd like to know why won't I!

MRS. BARTON. Because you're a Southern gentleman! [*Triumphantly, she sweeps out, taking* BABS *with her.*]

TUCKER. Wouldn't that—*curdle* you? A girl can do anything because she's a lady, but a fellow can't say anything because he's a gentleman!

UNCLE CLAIBOURNE. The double standard.

GIL. [*Off in distance.*] Hey, Tuck!

TUCKER. In here, Gil! Gosh! How'm I going to handle this? It's goin' to be an awful shock.

UNCLE CLAIBOURNE. Why not take him fishing?

TUCKER. Think he'd go with us?

UNCLE CLAIBOURNE. Allowin' a little time for moanin' and sighin' "lack and a day," I reckon he could be persuaded.

[GIL PRINGLE, *a likable youth with more brawn than brains, comes to the French windows.*]

GIL. Hey, Tucker, look! [*He stands posing in a modern sweater and dingy slacks combined with the cape, slouch hat, boots, sash and sword of a Civil War cavalry officer. Over his arm he carries the balance of the costume.*] Rhett Butler!

UNCLE CLAIBOURNE. To the life!

GIL. [*Anxiously.*] You think it's okay, huh? Mr. Twillinger says a wig and moustache'll make all the difference.

UNCLE CLAIBOURNE. I'm sure.

GIL. Anyway, it looks swell with Georgie's costume.

UNCLE CLAIBOURNE. [*To* TUCKER.] I'll go ask your mother

to put up some lunch. [*From door, Left.*] Remember—for shock, feet higher than head and an ice-bag on the brow. [*He goes out.*]

GIL. [*Busy at the mirror, trying various effects with his hat.*] Look, I don't know whether to wear it this way—over one eye—or sort of debonaire—like that. What do you think?

TUCKER. I think it couldn't matter less.

GIL. Sure it matters. I don't want to go with Georgie looking like a ghoul, do I? Not after her throwing over a Big Number just to go with me!

TUCKER. [*Outraged.*] When'd she tell you that?

GIL. Letter, yesterday. I can't show you all of it but— [*Carefully blocks off a portion.*]—you can read from there to there—

TUCKER. [*Reading.*] "Angel-cake: I'm turning down a B.D.—"

GIL. That's a Big Date.

TUCKER. "With an M.I.P.—"

GIL. That's a Most Important Person.

TUCKER. "—to go to the little ole Carnival with my wonderful B.F.—"

GIL. That's me. [BABS *re-enters, eating a doughnut.*] Looks like she's kind of crazy about me, don't you think? Turning down an M.I.P. to go with me! And over here—look where she says, "Love to my Sweeter 'n' Honey"—see all those crosses? Six of 'em!

BABS. Last time she only sent three.

GIL. You get out of here! [*He runs her out the French windows; comes back mooning over his letter again.*] "My Sweeter 'n' Honey"—what you starin' at?

TUCKER. You. If someone'd told me I wouldn't've believed it.

GIL. Huh?

TUCKER. Captain of the ball team! Best pitcher the school ever had! Gone googley over a fluff-brain!

GIL. Georgie isn't a fluff-brain!

TUCKER. And worse. If she weren't my own sister—and I weren't a gentleman, I'd call her a double-dating little digger.

GIL. Why, look here, you—! [*Starts for him,* TUCKER *dodges behind furniture.*] I've half a mind to give you a— [*Stops short.*] Why would you?

TUCKER. Why would I what?

GIL. Call her a—what you called her?

TUCKER. Because she *is* a double-dating little digger! [*Dodges behind couch as* GIL *clenches his fists.*] Now, wait until you hear! You think she's going with you to the Carnival but Mom's just got a special delivery. Georgie's going to a hop at the V.M.I.

GIL. What?

TUCKER. With her roommate's brother.

GIL. Why, the double-dating little— [*Throws his hat on the floor and jumps on it.*]

TUCKER. That's what I said.

GIL. [*His mood changing.*] She might have told me herself.

TUCKER. Not Georgie.

GIL. After all those crosses!

TUCKER. It's tough. [*After an instant's pause.*] Look, fellah, you aren't goin' to drool your life away just 'cause a femme gave you a raw deal! [*Instead of answering,* GIL *turns up toward French windows, stands back to room.* TUCKER *goes after him.*] You've got lots of good times ahead of you yet. Why, in twenty years bet you'll laugh when you think of this!

GIL. [*Brokenly.*] Twenty years isn't now.

TUCKER. I know. But look at it this way: there's lots of females steaming around. One of 'em'd be sure to run over you sooner or later. You got to learn to take 'em or leave 'em.

GIL. [*With a sigh.*] Reckon that's right.

TUCKER. Sure it's right. You ought to handle 'em the way I do. "Hello! Goodbye!" and then go fishin'. Say, there's an idea!

GIL. Where?

TUCKER. What's to keep you from goin' fishin'? Not a thing! Little ole foot-loose and fancy-free Pringle. That's you from now on!

GIL. But wait a minute—

TUCKER. Nothing to wait for! There's Uncle Clay's car standin' out there—[*A gesture toward French windows.*] —all ready to start.

GIL. I've got to return this costume.

TUCKER. We'll drop it off on the way. Gol-ly, it looks like a fine day for fish! All of 'em out ready an' waitin' for us! [*Goes through motions of casting, reeling, pulling in, etc.*] Whir—rr—rr! Hooked one! There he goes! Gosh, he's fighting!

GIL. [*Joining in.*] Looks like a three-pounder.

TUCKER. Not an ounce under five!

[GEORGIE BARTON *enters, Right. A year older than* TUCKER, *she is pretty enough to get away with murder. She stands holding a small handbag and watching the* BOYS.]

GIL. Look out! He's getting away!

TUCKER. Hand me the net—thanks. There! Landed him!

GEORGIE. [*Clapping.*] Nice work, Buddie!

TUCKER. What?
GIL. Who—?   } [*Together, swinging around.*]

GEORGIE. Just little ole me! [*Hugs* TUCKER.] My, oh mercy, it's good to see you! I declare to goodness you're gettin' right handsome!

TUCKER. Hey, lay off me! [*Wipes cheek.*] You're gooin' me up with lipstick!

GEORGIE. [*Abandoning him.*] Gil, precious, if you weren't afraid of lipstick—

GIL. [*A step toward her.*] I'm not!

TUCKER. [*Catching him back by his belt.*] But he can't stop now. We're going fishing.

GEORGIE. Fishing! Why, you're taking me to the Carnival tonight!

GIL. That's what I thought—

TUCKER. Until Mom got your special delivery.

GEORGIE. [*A trifle flatly.*] Oh, she got it!

TUCKER. She got it.

GEORGIE. I—I thought I'd reach here before *it* did.

TUCKER. That's what I thought you thought—*Lump of Sugar!*

GEORGIE. [*Talking brightly and rapidly to* GIL.] It doesn't really matter. Reckon I was out of my mind. My roommate's brother kept callin' an' callin' an' beggin' an' beggin' me to go with him until he plumb wore me down into sayin' that I would. But then I got to thinkin'—and of course I realized I wouldn't enjoy a minute—not the teeniest little minute—so we piled right into her car—

TUCKER. Who's car?
GIL. What car? } [*Together.*]

GEORGIE. Didn't I tell you? Shows you just how conflum-moxed I am! My new roommate's—Marylee Morse. She stopped to buy some flowers for Mother, but she'll be along in a minute.

TUCKER. Why? Her date go sour on her, too?

GEORGIE. I don't know what you're talkin' about. [*Quickly.*] Oh, Gil, is that your costume? I simply can't wait to see you in it! I know you'll look wonderful!

GIL. [*Fatuously, as he dusts off hat and puts it on, then takes pose.*] Rhett Butler.

GEORGIE. Oh, it's perfectly precious! Like I told you it would be in my letter!

TUCKER. You mean the letter you wrote Mom? Or the letter with all those crosses?

GEORGIE. [*Off-guard for a moment.*] Why—

TUCKER. [*Without waiting.*] Come on, fellah, we got to get started.

GEORGIE. Gil, honey—you aren't goin' with him? You wouldn't be that mean! [*Working hard.*] Not after my comin' home all special for the Carnival. You can go fishin' just as well next week—can't you?

GIL. [*Helplessly, to* TUCKER.] I can go fishin' next week— can't I?

TUCKER. Not with me, you can't! Listen, Sap, I'm tryin' to help you!

GIL. I don't need your help.

TUCKER. You just think you don't. It's like you were drowning—and I was a life-guard—and you were fighting me—

BABS. [*Popping in.*] Why don't you knock him out? [*As the two run her through the windows again.*] Well, that's what the life-guard does!

TUCKER. [*To* GIL, *as they come back in.*] You better make it snappy. I'm leaving with Uncle Clay in five minutes.

GEORGIE. Oh, no, you're not, Buddie. You're taking Marylee to the Carnival tonight.

TUCKER. You're batty!

GEORGIE. I know you haven't any other date—

TUCKER. You bet, I haven't any date—'cause I don't want any date. If I wanted a gal I'd get me a gal—[MARYLEE *enters from Right, carrying flowers and a box of candy. She is even prettier than* GEORGIE. GIL *tries to warn* TUCKER *who is going on with his tirade.*]—and she'd be a little Miss Luscious, not any old poison-pan with bow-legs an' buck-teeth—

GEORGIE. [*Grinning as she sees* MARYLEE.] How do you know she's got buck-teeth?

TUCKER. [*Cutting in on "she's got."*] Because that's the kind of a drizzle you'd pick for a roommate. [*Suddenly catches* GIL'S *frantic motions.*] Huh?

MARYLEE. Hello, ev'body!

TUCKER. [*Swings around—dazed.*] H—hello.

MARYLEE. The door was open so I walked right in. Hope you-all don't mind.

GEORGIE. No.

TUCKER. We don't mind. We don't mind at all. }[*Together.*]

GEORGIE. [*Speaking very fast.*] This is my brother Tucker, and this is Gil Pringle, but I guess I don't need to tell you that. You've been looking at his picture long enough on my bureau.

MARYLEE. [*Winningly, to* GIL.] And there's one on the wall, with that wonderful baseball team you're captain of. [*Transfers her dazzling smile to* TUCKER.] Georgie's got one of *you,* too, but it must have been taken a long time ago. It doesn't begin to do you justice.

TUCKER. [*Languishing.*] Doesn't it? [*Pulls himself together.*] If you'll excuse me I'll go find Mother—

GEORGIE. We'll find her. You go get our luggage from the car—[*A devastating look at* GIL.]—will you—Angel-cake?

GIL. [*To* TUCKER, *as they start out.*] Angel-cake!—Gosh!

MARYLEE. Oh—wait—I forgot— [TUCKER *comes back.*] The keys to my car. [*She holds them out, but as he reaches for them, she drops the chain. They* BOTH *bend over to pick them up. She gets them first.*] Oh! I'm just an ole clumsy! [*Presses them into his hand, making a play with her eyes.*] Here you are—Tucker.

TUCKER. Thanks—Marylee.

[*With difficulty, he tears himself away. The* GIRLS *hold their poses for a minute, then relax.*]

GEORGIE. Oh, darlin', you're *cosmic!*

MARYLEE. Think I started right?

GEORGIE. He took the bait, didn't he?

MARYLEE. [*Shaking her head.*] Isn't hooked yet.

GEORGIE. You wouldn't want it too easy. More fun when they fight.

MARYLEE. I don't see Gil fighting.

GEORGIE. No, the poor fish!

[*She takes up costume hat, puts it on her head in imitation of* GIL. *Giggles.* MARYLEE *giggles. The two fall on each other's necks, doing a wild dance and singing "There's a good time a-comin'!"* BABS *enters cautiously, sees the boys are not there, comes into the room.*]

BABS. Did your dates get the measles, too?

GEORGIE. What?

MARYLEE. What did you say? *[Together, stopping abruptly.]*

BABS. Johnny Jackson's sister couldn't go to the V.M.I. hop on account of it's been called off on account of the measles. I thought that was why you'd come home—

[She is choked off quickly by GEORGIE.*]*

GEORGIE. Hush up!

MARYLEE. *[With a sweet smile.]* We aren't mentioning that, honey.

GEORGIE. *[Improvising.]* We don't want to worry Mother.

BABS. Your mother?

MARYLEE. She's very nervous about infection.

GEORGIE. She wouldn't have a moment's peace if she knew.

MARYLEE. So we won't tell anyone—

GEORGIE. Not even the boys—

MARYLEE. Oh, no. Not even the boys.

BABS. *[Meaningly.]* Maybe *you* won't.

GEORGIE. Now listen, Babs, honey—

MARYLEE. *[Quickly.]* Sh!

GIL. *[Ambling in with a suitcase and bag.]* Here's your luggage.

TUCKER. *[Following.]* Where you want us to put it? *[Sees* BABS.*] You* in again?

GEORGIE. [*Quickly, puts arm over* BAB'S *shoulders.*] Why shouldn't she be in?

MARYLEE. We're just getting acquainted, aren't we, Babs?

GEORGIE. Here's a box of candy we brought for you, Babs.

TUCKER. You gone nuts?

BABS. [*Mistress of the situation.*] Thanks—but I'm reducing. I'd rather have—lipstick. [*Looks from one girl's lips to the other, indicates* MARYLEE.] I like hers best.

TUCKER. Why, you little moocher! ⎫
⎬ [*Together.*]
GIL. Where d'you think you get off— ⎭

MARYLEE. It's all right. I've got another— [*Hastily getting lipstick from her purse.*] There you are, honey.

BABS. Passion-pink! Oh, rapture! [*Starts out on the run, darts back again, picking up candy.*] I'll take this to Johnny Jackson. [*Out again.*]

GIL. [*The dawning of a faint suspicion.*] Say—what gives?

GEORGIE. Nothing. Nothing at all. Gil and I'll take those bags up, Buddie, while you show Marylee 'round. Come on, Gilly! I want to be sure my room is ready.

TUCKER. [*To* MARYLEE *as the* OTHERS *leave the room.*] Here's your key-chain. Gosh, that's a swell car you've got!

MARYLEE. [*Languishing.*] Do you really think so, Tucker?

TUCKER. I sure do! [*Another attempt to escape.*] Doesn't Mom know you're here yet? I'd better go find her—

MARYLEE. Wait a minute. [*He stops at Left.*] Not way over there—I want to tell you something.

TUCKER. [*Coming back.*] What is it?

MARYLEE. It's—oh, I declare, sayin' this comes mighty hard to a girl—but I couldn't help overhearin' what you said when I first came in.

TUCKER. Jeepers, I'm sorry!

MARYLEE. [*Quickly.*] Oh, I'm not blamin' *you,* Tucker. I wouldn't even mention it, only I want you to know it wasn't my idea—I mean about your takin' anybody like me to the Carnival. It was Georgie's.

TUCKER. Oh, I understand *that.*

MARYLEE. [*Earnestly.*] I'm mighty glad you do, because it would just about kill me if I thought you thought I was tryin' to force myself. Of course I know you must have dozens and hundreds of wonderful girls dyin' for you to date them.

TUCKER. [*Modestly.*] Oh, not *hundreds.*

MARYLEE. I wouldn't want you to blame Georgie, either. She was just feelin' sorry for me. I suppose a man like you can't understand how it is with a girl, but she can't help bein' just a little bit silly about a picture she sees when she first opens her eyes every morning and closes her eyes every night.

TUCKER. [*Going overboard.*] Can't she—Marylee?

MARYLEE. No. And when I hinted so terribly about Georgie bringin' me home with her—well, I suppose she thought she just had to try to force me onto you, but you do understand it wasn't my idea—don't you, Tucker?

TUCKER. Sure, I do!

MARYLEE. And you'll pretend it never happened, and go right on and date Miss Luscious, or whatever her name is—

TUCKER. I wasn't dating any girl—honest I wasn't. I was just going fishing.

MARYLEE. [*In thrilling tones.*] *Fishing!*

TUCKER. Do you like to fish?

MARYLEE. Like to fish? It's my idea of heaven! Baiting the hook, and throwing it into the water—and then pulling out all those lovely, beautiful—salmon!

TUCKER. These are trout.

MARYLEE. Oh, I like trout much better! They're my favorite fish!

TUCKER. They're mine, too. [*Solemnly.*] Gosh, that's a coincidence—isn't it?

MARYLEE. It sure 'nuff is!

TUCKER. It makes you think. I mean, it almost seems as if it *meant* something.

MARYLEE. It sure 'nuff does! [*In a different tone.*] When are you leaving?

TUCKER. Leaving?

MARYLEE. To go fishing.

TUCKER. I *was* leaving right away, but now—

MARYLEE. [*Breaking in on "away."*] And I've been keeping you from starting!

TUCKER. There's no hurry!

MARYLEE. But there *is*! If you don't get off it'll be too late. Tell you what—because you've been so heavenly sweet—I'm going to let you take my car.

TUCKER. Oh, I couldn't do that.

MARYLEE. 'Course you could! I won't be needing it. Really-truly I won't. [*Oh! so bravely.*] I'll just see Georgie and Gil off to the Carnival, then I'll spend a nice quiet evening at home—with your mother. You go right ahead and take these keys— [*Makes pretense of pressing them on him, same business of dropping, picking up, etc.*] Heavenly Day, there I go again! Reckon I've got ten thumbs!

TUCKER. Let me see! [*Takes hands, looks at them.*] Gosh, you've got pretty hands, Marylee!

MARYLEE. Do you think so, Tucker?

TUCKER. And your lashes—you could tie 'em in bow-knots!

MARYLEE. You do tell the prettiest lies!

TUCKER. But I'm not! You could! Honest!

GEORGIE. [*Comes downstairs with* GIL *on cue "could."*] Everything's ready upstairs, but the boys forgot your hat-box.

TUCKER. I'll get it for you, Marylee.

MARYLEE. It's full of perfume. You'll be mighty careful of it—won't you—honey?

TUCKER. [*Fairly singing the name.*] I sure 'nuff will—

Marylee! [*He stumbles out, looking back idiotically over his shoulder.*]

GIL. [*Gazes after him with growing suspicion.*] Say—what you done to him—huh?

MARYLEE. Not a thing!

MRS. BARTON. [*Entering Left with basket.*] Here's your lunch, boys— Why, Georgie!

GEORGIE. Hello, Momsy!

MRS. BARTON. Why didn't somebody tell me?

GEORGIE. No time. My, you look wonderful! This is my roommate, Marylee Morse. I brought her with me.

MRS. BARTON. That's nice! But what are you doing home? I thought that you—

GEORGIE. [*Hurriedly, on "I thought."*] Aren't you glad to see us? We figured you'd be tickled.

MARYLEE. [*Also hurriedly, on cue "you'd be."*] Here are some flowers for you, Mrs. Barton.

MRS. BARTON. [*Distractedly, her hands full of the flowers and the lunch basket.*] Why, thank you—they're lovely. But I thought you were both going to the hop.

GEORGIE. [*On cue "going."*] We changed our minds. Isn't Gil's costume wonderful? I do hope you arranged about mine. Scarlet O'Hara. You got Scarlet O'Hara for me, didn't you, darling?

MRS. BARTON. Yes, I did. I mean, I didn't. I mean, I called Mr. Twillinger and cancelled it after I got your special delivery letter—

GEORGIE. [*Very, very gaily.*] Then you'll just have to call Mr. Twillinger and *un*cancel it. I'm going to take Marylee upstairs to my room.

MARYLEE. I'm plumb filthy. [*Shakes immaculate skirts.*] Just look at the dust!

MRS. BARTON. But, oh dear, I've called so many times. I do hate to call again—

GEORGIE. [*Starting for stairs.*] Tell him the Scarlet O'Hara for me—and a dress for Marylee—the one with the ruffles going 'round and 'round. [*Same gesture as her mother's.*]

MARYLEE. [*From stairs.*] And don't forget—a costume for Tucker.

MRS. BARTON. Tucker!

GEORGIE. Oh, yes. Get a costume for Tucker.

MRS. BARTON. Georgie! Come back here! Georgie! [*But the* GIRLS *are already upstairs.* MRS. BARTON *puts down her basket and the flowers, crosses to telephone speaking to* GIL.] I didn't catch why they'd changed their minds about the V.M.I. Did you?

GIL. [*Thoughtfully.*] I sure didn't.

MRS. BARTON. [*Dialing to a burst of girlish laughter from upstairs.*] 3—9—3, no! 9—3—9, Oh, dear, I'm so flustered! Good morning, Mr. Barton, this is Mrs. Twillinger. I mean this is Mrs.— Oh, you recognized my voice! Well, I'm not a mite surprised!

UNCLE CLAIBOURNE. [*Enters from Left, tackle and fishing boots in hand; a disreputable straw hat on the back of his head.*] What's all that high palamity goin' on upstairs?

GIL. Girls.

UNCLE CLAIBOURNE. No!

GIL. Uh-huh.

MRS. BARTON. Sh! [*Into telephone.*] I called to ask you to forget the last time I called—I mean when I said we didn't want that dress with the ruffles running 'round and 'round—[*Gestures with hand.*] Yes. Now we *do* want it for my daughter's roommate. And the Scarlet O'Hara, too— Yes—

UNCLE CLAIBOURNE. What happened to good old V.M.I.?

GIL. You askin' *me?*

MRS. BARTON. [*Still into telephone.*] And while you're looking, you might find something for Tucker— Yes, Tucker—

[UNCLE CLAIBOURNE *stares at* GIL *who nods his head. While* MRS. BARTON *continues to murmur into the telephone* TUCKER *enters from Right. He is carrying a transparent plastic hat-box tied with a large satin bow as though it is made of Venetian glass and contains crown jewels instead of perfume flasks. His eyes are on the box so that he does not notice the* GIRLS *are missing.*]

TUCKER. Here's your hat-box, Marylee. I haven't spilled a drop! [*Stops, looks around.*] Where is she? [GIL *points upward without speaking.* TUCKER *starts for stairs, still at the same careful gait.*] Mary-lee-yee!

MRS. BARTON. Tucker, wait! Mr. Twillinger says would you rather be Henry the Eighth or a Confederate General?

TUCKER. What's Marylee going to wear?

MRS. BARTON. Hoop skirts.

TUCKER. Confederate, of course. Oh, Mary—lee—yee!

UNCLE CLAIBOURNE. [*As* TUCKER *bleats his way upstairs.*] I'll be eternally whang-dangled! [*Flings his hat; it sails over the couch and falls behind it.*]

MRS. BARTON. [*Into telephone.*] Yes, that will do nicely. Thank you so much—goodbye! [*Rises and starts Left.*] I've thought of a wonderful idea! I'm going to polish Great Grandfather's sword for Tucker to wear.

UNCLE CLAIBOURNE. Wear to what? [*To* GIL *as* MRS. BARTON *goes off.*] What's going on around here? I'm out of the room three-four minutes and when I get back— [*Breaks off and sniffs.*] You smell what I smell?

GIL. I'll say I do!

TUCKER. [*Coming downstairs in a bemused fashion.*] It's *Love Dream.*

UNCLE CLAIBOURNE. It's what?

TUCKER. *Love Dream.* She put some on my cuff. Marylee did.

UNCLE CLAIBOURNE. Well now, the fish are certainly goin' to love that!

TUCKER. [*Vaguely.*] Fish?

UNCLE CLAIBOURNE. Fish. Those silver things with fins and tails. The ones you were going to catch on a hook.

TUCKER. Oh, yes, fish. Well, uh—I was going to explain about that—

UNCLE CLAIBOURNE. You don't need to.

TUCKER. H'm?

UNCLE CLAIBOURNE. When a male adolescent walks downstairs backward with an expression like that on his face and a smell like that on his cuff— [*A sudden roar of wrath.*] By hookey! I'd be afraid to *let* you go fishin'! You'd get took for a worm!

TUCKER. [*Dreamily.*] She likes to fish. Marylee does.

UNCLE CLAIBOURNE. I can see that with half an eye.

TUCKER. She even offered to let me go fishing in her car. Look—there's her key-chain.

GIL. You mean *ball* and chain.

TUCKER. What?

GIL. [*In sudden decision.*] I don't like it. I don't like it a-tall!

TUCKER. Don't like what?

GIL. I don't know what. That's what I don't like.

UNCLE CLAIBOURNE. You catch a faint fishy odor—h'm?

GIL. You said it! Ask me—there's a skunk in the woodpile!

MRS. BARTON. [*Off.*] Uncle Clay! Come help me get down this sword, will you? I can't reach.

UNCLE CLAIBOURNE. Coming! Don't you boys do anythin' important 'til I get back! [*Exits Left.*]

GIL. [*To* TUCKER *who is still lost in a dream.*] See here. I been doin' some thinkin'. [TUCKER *discovers one of the flowers dropped from the bouquet, picks it up.*] I wouldn't have done it if it hadn't been for what you said yourself—

TUCKER. I said?

GIL. Little while ago. About letting females run over you and ruin your life.

TUCKER. Oh, that. Did you notice her hair? Marylee's?

GIL. What about it?

TUCKER. It's the kind of a color—well—it's the kind of a color that you might say—looks *best* on her.

GIL. Jumping Jehoshaphat!

TUCKER. And her eyes—they're that kind of a color, too.

GIL. [*Earnestly.*] Listen, fellah. You got to listen to me, 'bout what I was thinkin'. I was thinkin', what've I got Friday I didn't have Thursday? What I mean—if Georgie wants to go with me to the Carnival on Wednesday, and with another Joe on Thursday, and with me again on Friday—I say to myself, "What's happened to that other Joe?"

TUCKER. [*Still dazed.*] Joe who?

GIL. Didn't you hear a word I said?

TUCKER. You were talking about Joe somebody.

GIL. [*A howl of exasperation.*] Aw! [*Controls himself, explains as he might talk to a child of three.*] Look! Pull yourself together and answer this. Just try an' answer. What happened to the Joe that was going to take Georgie to the V.M.I.? And what happened to the other Joe—

TUCKER. Two Joes?

GIL. The Joe that was going to take Marylee?

TUCKER. [*Simply.*] Why—nothing.

GIL. [*As* UNCLE CLAIBOURNE *re-enters.*] Then why'd Georgie decide to come home? Why'd this Marylee character come with her?

TUCKER. Because of my photograph on her dresser.

GIL. What?

TUCKER. [*Dreamily.*] Every morning when she first closed her eyes and every night when she opened them—so she got good old Georgie to bring her—

GIL. Who told you that?

TUCKER. [*Putting everything into the name.*] Mary—lee.

GIL. [*Disgustedly, to* UNCLE CLAIBOURNE.] Look at him. Just *look* at him!

UNCLE CLAIBOURNE. He's sure the mess of this world!

[BABS *enters, carrying the candy box and the lipstick. She stalks down Right and slaps them smartly on the table. Her lips are richly crimson.*]

BABS. Will you please to kindly tell the girls that I don't accept bribes on account of I'm not a blackmailer?

GIL. [*Not really listening.*] Sure, we'll tell 'em. [*To* TUCKER.] Now, you listen to me— [*Suddenly, turns on* BABS.] *What* did you say?

BABS. I said I'm not a blackmailer and anyway Mother won't let me keep the lipstick. You can furthermore tell 'em I'm not a blab-mouth. If Mrs. Barton gets scared it won't be by me.

GIL. Scared?

UNCLE CLAIBOURNE. Scared of what? } [*Together.*]

BABS. Those measles at the V.M.I.

UNCLE CLAIBOURNE. That bangs it!

BABS. That's why they had to call off the hop.

GIL. [*To* TUCKER.] I told you!

TUCKER. I don't believe it!

BABS. You can ask Johnny Jackson's sister.

GIL. You bet I will!

TUCKER. I don't mean I don't believe about the measles. I don't believe that's why the girls came home.

GIL. You wouldn't believe in elephants if one was sittin' on you!

TUCKER. They could have made up their minds before the dance was called off.

UNCLE CLAIBOURNE. And I could grow six legs.

[*The* GIRLS *are heard laughing and talking, off.*]

GIL. [*To* UNCLE CLAIBOURNE.] Can't you find some way to prove it to him?

BABS. Prove what, Buddie?

GIL. You get out!

UNCLE CLAIBOURNE. And take your loot with you!

BABS. [*Wailing, as they run her out, candy, lipstick and all.*] What have *I* done?

GIL. And *stay* out!

MARYLEE. [*Off.*] Oh, Georgie, I do think your house is divine, simply divine!

GEORGIE. [*Off.*] It's just a little ole ordinary house.

MARYLEE. [*Off.*] And I think your family is divine, too! [*She comes downstairs followed by* GEORGIE, *stops in pretty confusion.*] Mercy me! I hope nobody was listenin' to what I said!

UNCLE CLAIBOURNE. Nobody but little ole us.

MARYLEE. I know who *you* are! You're Uncle Claibourne. Tucker. I know you from seeing your picture—

UNCLE CLAIBOURNE. On Georgie's dresser.

MARYLEE. In her mem'ry book.

UNCLE CLAIBOURNE. Where you looked at it every mornin' and night.

GEORGIE. [*Quickly.*] Uncle Clay is a terrible tease.

MARYLEE. Don't you suppose I *know* that? [*Using her eyes on him.*] Seems like I haven't heard much else since I moved in with Georgie except those marvelously clever things you're always sayin'.

UNCLE CLAIBOURNE. Could you quote me a few?

GEORGIE. [*Quickly.*] Don't be a silly-dilly! Haven't you boys gone for our costumes yet?

TUCKER. Not yet.

MARYLEE. Let's all run down in my car. [*Taking* TUCKER'S *arm.*] You can drive.

GEORGIE. Bring your costume, Gil. We'll try everything on down there.

GIL. Wait a minute—

UNCLE CLAIBOURNE. [*Interrupting him.*] Fine idea! If you don't mind, I'll ride downtown with you. I want to buy some fish.

GEORGIE. Fish?

UNCLE CLAIBOURNE. Your mother was counting on a mess of trout. Looks like I'll have to buy it—unless fish disagrees with you, Miss Marylee?

MARYLEE. [*Surprised.*] Why, no. No, it doesn't.

UNCLE CLAIBOURNE. That's good. Some folks, it does. Now where'd I put my hat? Some folks can't eat fish without breakin' out all over in spots—like the measles.

GEORGIE. [*Caught by the word.*] Measles?

UNCLE CLAIBOURNE. Mm. [*Improvising.*] Especially upon eating the Spratitorius Investigorium—a fish like the ordinary pike or pickerel except that it has ten gills instead of only seven. See my hat over there anywhere?

GIL. Isn't here.

UNCLE CLAIBOURNE. [*Still searching.*] Yes, sir! Let one little Spraticus get mixed up with a mess of other fish—he'll break out the folks that eat him into every kind of spots there is— like this business up at V.M.I.

GEORGIE. What business?

UNCLE CLAIBOURNE. Didn't you hear 'bout that? Here's my hat! Knew I'd put it somewhere. Well—nothing to keep us —come on!

GEORGIE. [*Not moving.*] But what happened—

MARYLEE. At V.M.I.?

UNCLE CLAIBOURNE. Did I say V.M.I.? Now, maybe it was M.I.T. Allus did get 'em mixed. Whichever, it was the one was giving a hop. Certainly would have saved a lot of trouble if the V.M.I. boys—or M.I.T. boys had known about those little Spraticusses and what they could do to you. Yes, sir! Would have saved 'em the trouble invitin' their girls, then disinvitin' 'em—then tryin' to invite 'em again when, like enough, they'd gone home or were otherwise hard to get hold of. Aren't you coming?

TUCKER. Sure. Come on, Marylee.

MARYLEE. [*Slightly distracted.*] In a minute— [*She and* GEORGIE *exchange worried glances.*] If—if I'm going to try on my costume I ought to take my makeup kit along—don't you think?

GEORGIE. I certainly do. And I want to get some petticoats.

MARYLEE. [*Following her quickly toward stairs.*] Me, too! You don't mind waiting, do you, Tucker?

TUCKER. No, I don't mind.

GEORGIE. [*As they go off.*] We won't take long.

UNCLE CLAIBOURNE. [*To the* BOYS.] Just long enough to put in a call on the upstairs extension!

TUCKER. A call?

GIL. Sure. To the V.M.I.—to find out if the dance is on again.

UNCLE CLAIBOURNE. They'll find out, all right. [*Chuckles.*] Spraticus Investigorium! Pretty good, h'm?

TUCKER. You mean, you made all that up?

UNCLE CLAIBOURNE. What do you think? [*To* GIL.] I'll bring the lunch. You fetch his gear.

TUCKER. What you talkin' about?

GIL. [*Picking up fishing gear and hat.*] Never mind, sonny.

TUCKER. Now, wait a minute—

MRS. BARTON. [*Enters, carrying a newly-shined sword and scabbard.*] Here's Great Grandfather's sword for Tucker.

UNCLE CLAIBOURNE. That'll be just fine for cuttin' up bait.

MRS. BARTON. Bait! You aren't going fishing!

GIL. We sure are!

UNCLE CLAIBOURNE. You bet!

TUCKER. I didn't say I was going.

UNCLE CLAIBOURNE. You don't need to.

GIL. We're going to save you from yourself.

MRS. BARTON. What are you talking about?

UNCLE CLAIBOURNE. [*Still to* TUCKER.] If it'll make you easier in your mind— [*Picks up telephone, speaks into it.*] Hello, Central—about that call to V.M.I.—the one we just placed. How long will it take? [*Holds receiver so* TUCKER *can hear.*] Oh, you're putting it right through! That's all I want to know. Thanks!

[TUCKER *sags onto couch, but is pulled up by* GIL, *who slaps his hat down over his forehead, then tugs on one arm while* UNCLE CLAIBOURNE *pulls on the other.*]

GIL. Come on, fellah!

UNCLE CLAIBOURNE. Make it snappy!

MRS. BARTON. [*As they reach the French windows.*] But wait—I don't understand—what am I to tell the girls?

UNCLE CLAIBOURNE. Tell them goodbye!

GIL. Tell them we've got a B.D. with an M.I.P.

TUCKER. [*Suddenly recovering.*] Tell 'em to go break out in pink spots! [*Grabbing his hat off his head he waves it.*] Yippee! [*Jams it on the back of his head, goes out the French windows.*]

MRS. BARTON. Oh, dear—oh, Mercy Goodness!

[*The* GIRLS *run down stairs.*]

MARYLEE. All ready, Tucker, honey!

GEORGIE. Here I am, Gil! Why—where're the boys?

MRS. BARTON. Gone fishing.

MARYLEE. Fishing! ⎫
                            ⎬ [*Together.*]
GEORGIE. Gone fishing! ⎭

MRS. BARTON. [*Starting for telephone.*] Fishing.

MARYLEE. Oh, no!

GEORGIE. They can't! Don't let them! [*Sound of motor starting, off. Both* GIRLS *run to the French windows, calling, while* MRS. BARTON *wearily dials that number.*] Gil! Wait! Gil!

MARYLEE. Tucker! Tucker, honey!

MRS. BARTON. —9—3—9—

GEORGIE. Don't go! Please don't go!

MARYLEE. Come back!

[*Sounds of a barber-shop trio singing* "Goodnight, Ladies" *off.* GIRLS *go out, calling.*]

MRS. BARTON. [*Into telephone.*] Southern Costume? Mr. Twillinger? This is—guess who! That's right! [*As Curtain starts slowly down.*] I'm dreadfully sorry, but it seems there was a little mistake about tonight. Yes— [GIRLS *come back in, defeated.*] I guess *maybe* we won't be needing those costumes—

CURTAIN

THE TRIUMPH OF JOB

A Pageant-Play in One Act

Adapted from *The Book of Job*

BY

FLORENCE RYERSON

CHARACTERS

FIRST NARRATOR
SECOND NARRATOR
JOB
JOB'S WIFE
A HERDSMAN
A CAMEL-DRIVER
A SHEPHERD
A MESSENGER
ELIPHAZ
BILDAD
ZOPHAR
THE VOICE OF JEHOVAH
AN OLD WOMAN
A RICH MAN

Also: Job's sons, daughters and grandchildren; dancing girls, villagers, slaves, shepherds, street urchins, etc.

TIME

Several centuries before the birth of Christ.

PLACE

A town in the land of Uz.

SCENES

Prologue: Before the curtain.
Scene 1: The House of Job. Day and Night.
Scene 2: Outside the gates of the city. Day and Night.

FOREWORD

The Book of Job is as old as the hills, as new as tomorrow's sunrise.

The questions which Job asked of his friends, of his soul, of his God, have been asked at one time or another by every man or woman who has been forced to witness today's apparently meaningless martyrdom not only of innocent individuals but of whole races.

The purpose of this adaptation is to compress and clarify the diffuse and sometimes contradictory Biblical material and bring the whole into a form which will make stage presentation possible.

Because of limitations of time, and because a modern audience refuses to listen to over-long speeches, drastic cuts have been made, the material rearranged, and individual speeches of Zophar, Eliphaz and Bildad have been divided among the three. An element of pageantry has also been introduced along with short excerpts from the Psalms, but every attempt has been made to retain the word-beauty and spirit of the great original.

Those organizations whose resources forbid full production with the sets, costumes and musical interludes indicated in the script will find this arrangement easily adaptable for simpler production against curtains. It is also suitable for group, radio, and television readings.

THE TRIUMPH OF JOB

Prologue

Before the Curtain

TWO NARRATORS *enter from Left and Right. They wear long dark robes with large cowls which shadow their faces.*

FIRST NARRATOR. There was a man in the land of Uz, whose name was Job: and that man was perfect and upright, one that loved God, and turned away from evil, the greatest of all men of the East.

SECOND NARRATOR. There were born to him seven sons and three daughters. His sons feasted in their houses, everyone upon his day. They sent for their sisters to eat and drink with them. Upon the day of their feasting Job arose early in the morning and offered burnt-offerings for he said, "It may be that my sons have sinned in their hearts."

FIRST NARRATOR. Thus did Job continually, for he was clothed in righteousness.

SECOND NARRATOR. Now there was a day when the heavenly hosts came to present themselves before Jehovah, and Satan came with them. The Lord said, "From whence comest thou?"

FIRST NARRATOR. Satan answered: "From going to and fro in the earth, and from walking up and down therein."

SECOND NARRATOR. And the Lord said unto Satan, "Hast thou considered my servant, Job? There is none like him, a perfect and an upright man, one that loveth God and turneth away from all evil."

FIRST NARRATOR. Satan answered: "Doth Job love God for naught? Thou hast blessed the work of his hands and increased his substance in the land. But put forth thy hand, now, touch all that he hath; he will curse thee to thy face."

[*The lights begin to dim.*]

SECOND NARRATOR. The Lord said unto Satan, "Behold, all that Job hath is in thy power; only, upon himself do not lay thy hand."

[*The* SECOND NARRATOR *moves to Left of stage, the* FIRST NARRATOR *to the Right, during the following speech.*]

FIRST NARRATOR. There came a day when Job's sons and daughters were about him— [*His voice dies away. The Curtains part.*]

Scene I

TIME: *Day.*

SCENE: *The main room of Job's dwelling. Although the master is a wealthy man, the room is simple, its principal beauty being in its rugs, hangings and pottery.*

There are no windows but a sunlit courtyard garden is visible through open doors upper Center. The main entrance from the street is at Left, balanced by the suggestion of a family altar at Right. A number of weapons, bows, arrows, knives and spears are carelessly piled near the door.

At Rise: A meal is in progress. JOB, *a fine, vigorous man in his late middle-age, is seated at Center. To Left and Right are* JOB'S *seven sons with various friends. His* WIFE, *his* DAUGHTERS, *and his* SONS' WIVES, *are serving their men folk with dishes which are brought in by servants.*

Several pretty CHILDREN, *members of the family, are dancing to music supplied by a harpist or flutist, a slave with castanets, and one with a tambourine or small drum. The lights are bright, costumes gay, the whole scene full of happiness and well-being.*

The CHILDREN *finish their dance. The ensuing laughter and applause are interrupted by violent knocking on the door Left.*

HERDSMAN. [*Calling, off.*] Master! Master! [*A* SERVANT *unbars the door. The* HERDSMAN *runs in. His clothing is torn and he is bleeding from a wound on his forehead.*] Master! Thy oxen were plowing and thy asses feeding beside them. The Sabeans fell upon them and carried them away! They have slain thy servants with the edge of the sword! I, only, have escaped to tell thee!

[*He collapses. There is immediate excitement.* JOB'S SONS *and several* MALE SERVANTS *hurry to arm themselves while* JOB *and the* WOMEN *go to the aid of the wounded man. The* SONS *and* SERVANTS *rush out, brandishing their weapons.* JOB'S WIFE *brings him a goblet from the table which he holds to the* HERDSMAN'S *lips.*]

CAMEL-DRIVER. [*From off in the distance.*] Master! Master!

[*A* CAMEL-DRIVER *and a* SHEPHERD *appear in the arch of the door which has been left open by the sons when they rushed out.* BOTH *are exhausted, their faces blackened and their clothing charred as though by fire.*] Master!—thy camels!

The fire of God is fallen from heaven! It has burned thy camels!

SHEPHERD. It has killed all thy sheep!

[*The* WOMEN *moan in horror and despair.* ALL *turn toward* JOB.]

JOB. [*Gently.*] Shall we receive good at the hands of God, and shall we not receive evil?

[*He turns slowly Right toward the family altar as the lights dim down to blackness. Sounds of a wind in the distance which continue through next scene.*]

FIRST NARRATOR. [*From the side of the proscenium.*] And Job sinned not, nor charged God foolishly, but behold, that night, there came a great wind from the wilderness. A messenger came unto Job.

JOB'S VOICE. [*In the darkness.*] All the while my breath is in me,
And the spirit of God is in my nostrils,
My lips shall not speak wickedness,
Nor my tongue utter deceit.
[*Lights go up slowly, disclosing* JOB *before the altar. His* WIFE *is also in the room with a few* WOMEN SERVANTS. *A slow, ominous knock is heard. The* WOMEN *look at the door, afraid to open it.* JOB *continues his worship.*]
Till I die I will not remove mine integrity from me.
My righteousness I will hold fast.
My heart shall not reproach me so long as I live.

[*The knock is repeated.* JOB *turns as the door is opened slowly from without. A* MESSENGER *enters. He wears dark colors, is evidently in deep grief.*]

MESSENGER. Master! Thy sons and thy daughters—

JOB. [*Fearfully, as the man's voice fails.*] My sons?

JOB'S WIFE. [*Almost in a whisper.*] My daughters?

MESSENGER. They were eating and drinking in the house of the eldest. A great wind came and smote the corners of the house— [*Again his voice fails.*] I only have escaped.

JOB'S WIFE. [*Wildly, to her husband.*] Curse God! Curse God and let us die!

JOB. [*Stands for a moment, fighting for self-control, then he pulls himself together, raises his head. Slowly—with obvious effort.*] The Lord gave, and the Lord hath taken away; blessed be the name of the Lord.

CURTAIN

[*The* NARRATORS *move forward again.*]

FIRST NARRATOR. And still Job sinned not, nor charged God foolishly.

SECOND NARRATOR. And there was a day when the heavenly hosts came again to present themselves before Jehovah and Satan came also. The Lord said unto Satan, "From whence comest thou?"

FIRST NARRATOR. Satan answered, "From going to and fro in the earth and from walking up and down therein."

SECOND NARRATOR. And the Lord said unto Satan, "Hast thou considered my servant, Job? Although thou moved me against him, to destroy him without cause, still he holds fast his integrity. Surely there is none like him on earth."

FIRST NARRATOR. Satan answered the Lord: "All that a man hath will he give for his life. But put forth thine hand now, touch his bone and flesh. He will curse thee to thy face."

SECOND NARRATOR. And the Lord said unto Satan, "He is in thine hand; but preserve his life."

FIRST NARRATOR. So Satan went forth from the presence of the Lord, and smote Job with boils from the sole of his foot to the crown of his head. [NARRATORS *move back to sides of proscenium as the Curtains part.*] Job took a potsherd to scrape himself and sat down among the ashes without the gates of the city.

SCENE II

Day. Outside the village gates. Center back, a length of wall, the suggestion of an arch. A well-head at Left with a few crude water jars. At Right, a circle of stones about the ashes of a dead fire.

Since this is a public place, men are seated by the outer wall at Left. VILLAGERS *come and go. In addition to the action specified in the script they are busy carrying wood, water, spinning thread, or just sitting and loafing during all of the following scenes. This should be done in such a way that we feel* JOB *and his friends are part of the communal life and that the former draws inspiration for many of his speeches from what goes on about him.*

At Rise: JOB *is seated by the dead fire. He now wears dark clothing, shabby and dusted with ashes. He has aged. His hair shows grey. His* WIFE, *also dressed somberly, stands at the Right, watching him, worried and unhappy. The* VILLAGERS, *are at Left, all busy with their own affairs.*

FIRST NARRATOR. [*Continuing while Curtains are parting.*] Now when Job's three friends heard of the evil which had fallen upon him they made an appointment together and came, each from his own place, to mourn with Job and comfort him. [*The* THREE MEN *enter from the Left.* ELIPHAZ *is a few years younger than* JOB, *dressed colorfully.* BILDAD *is* JOB'S *age, with a square black beard.* ZOPHAR *is much older, near-sighted and rather deaf.* ALL *give the impression of having traveled some distance.*] But when they saw him they knew him not.

[*The three are about to pass* JOB *without recognition when his* WIFE *hurries toward them.*]

JOB'S WIFE. [*Stopping them and greeting them.*] Eliphaz! Bildad and Zophar!

[*She indicates her husband with a gesture. They are plainly horrified by his appearance.*]

SECOND NARRATOR. They lifted up their voices and wept. Then they sat down with him upon the ground, but none spake a word unto him; for they saw that his grief was very great.

[JOB'S FRIENDS *sit down to Left and Right upon the stones around the dead fire.* JOB'S WIFE *goes through the gate into the city, but* JOB *does not seem to see what is going on around him. After a moment he speaks, as though to himself.*]

JOB. Let the day perish wherein I was born,
And the night which said, "There is a man child conceived."
Let that day be darkness, and the shadow of death be upon it.
Let the stars of the twilight thereof be dark;
Let it look for light, but have none,
Because it hid not sorrow from mine eyes.

ELIPHAZ. If we commune with thee, wilt thou be grieved?

JOB. [*Still to himself, not answering* ELIPHAZ.] Why died
 I not from the womb?
For now should I have lain still and been quiet.
I should have slept and been at rest
With kings and counsellors of the earth.

[*An* OLD WOMAN *comes from the gate, crosses to the well
with her water jar.*]

Wherefore is light given to him that is in misery,
And life unto the bitter in soul,
Which long for death, but it cometh not;
Which rejoice exceedingly, and are glad,
When they can find the grave?

BILDAD. [*To the* OTHERS.] Who can withhold himself from
 speaking?

JOB. There the wicked cease from troubling,
There the weary are at rest.

[*Three or four* PRISONERS *with heavy burdens come through
from the Right, and go into the city gate. They are followed
by a cruel-looking* TASKMASTER.]

There the prisoners rest together,
They hear not the voice of the oppressor.
The small and great are there,
And the servant is free from his master.

[*Several* GIRLS *come out through the gate carrying jars.
They go to the well, push aside the* OLD WOMAN *and fill
their jars.*]

When I lie down I say,
"When shall I arise and the night be gone?"
I am full of tossing to and fro

Until the dawning of the day.
I remember that my life is wind,
Mine eye shall no more see good,
For the thing which I greatly feared is come upon me.

ELIPHAZ. Thou hast instructed many,
Thou hast strengthened the weak hands,
Thy words have upheld him that was falling.
But now trouble comes upon thee and thou faintest;
It touches thee and thou art frightened.

[ELIHU, *a fine-looking young chap enters through gate,
crosses to well, helps the* OLD WOMAN *fill her jar.*]

BILDAD. Man is born to trouble as the sparks fly upward.

ZOPHAR. We are but of yesterday and know nothing.

JOB. Yea, man born of woman is of few days and full of
    trouble.
He comes forth like a flower, and is cut down,
He flees as a shadow and continues not.
Have pity ! Have pity upon me, oh my friends,
For the hand of the Almighty has touched me.
My days are past, my purposes are broken off,
Even the thoughts of my heart. [*Rises.*]
What is my strength that I should hope?
What is mine end, that I should prolong life?

[*Gaily dressed* DANCING GIRLS *enter from gate, flirt with*
LOAFERS *and try to attract young* ELIHU'S *attention. He
ignores them.*]

ELIPHAZ. Affliction comes not forth from the dust,
Neither does trouble spring from the ground.

BILDAD. [*Rising.*] Does God pervert judgment?

Does the Almighty pervert justice?
With him are all strength and wisdom.

ZOPHAR. Let not him that is deceived trust in vanity,
For vanity shall be his recompense.

JOB. [*Humbly.*] If I have walked with vanity,
If my foot has hastened to deceit,
If I have rejoiced because my wealth was great,
Or at the destruction of him that hated me,
Then let mine arm fall from my shoulder blade,
For these things were iniquity to be punished by God.

[*A* DANCING GIRL *comes Right and mockingly jingles her
coin necklace before* JOB *who draws away, regarding her
sternly.*]

I have made a covenant with mine eyes;
Why then should I think upon a maid?

[*She laughs and goes back toward Left.*]

Oh, let me be weighed in an even balance
That God may know mine integrity!
My foot has held to God's steps;
His ways I have kept and not declined;
He knows that my prayer is pure;
Yet he has kindled his wrath against me.
And counts me as one of his enemies.

ELIPHAZ. Surely if thou wert pure and upright,
God would awake for thee
And make the habitations of thy righteousness prosper!

ZOPHAR. God will not cast away a perfect man.

BILDAD. Neither will he help the evil doer.

ELIPHAZ. He exacts less of thee than thine iniquity deserves.

JOB. Miserable comforters are ye all!
I am as one mocked of his neighbour,
Who calls upon God and he answers him not!
The just upright man is laughed to scorn
While the tents of the robbers prosper.
They that provoke God are secure.

ZOPHAR. [*Rises, frightened by such heresy.*] How long wilt
thou speak these things?
How long shall thy words be like a strong wind
Turning thy spirit against God?

[*A little troop of* SHEPHERDS *enter from Right. One is
carrying a small lamb or kid, wrapped in a shawl. Another
leads a shepherd dog. They cross and go out Left.* ZOPHAR
approaches JOB, *placatingly.*]

ZOPHAR. Whoever perished being innocent?

BILDAD. Or where were the righteous cut off?

JOB. Behold! All ye yourselves have seen it!
The wicked remove the landmarks;
They take away flocks
And turn the needy out of the way;
They cause the naked to lodge without clothing
So that they have no covering in the cold.
They pluck the fatherless from the breast
And take away the sheaf from the hungry;
Yet God lays not wickedness to them.

ELIPHAZ. [*To* BILDAD.] He puts no trust in the Holy One!

BILDAD. The heavens themselves are not clean in his
sight!

ZOPHAR. [*Sternly, to* JOB.] When thou mockest, shall no
    man make thee ashamed?
The wicked man travails with pain all his days,
A dreadful sound is in his ears.
He knows that the day of darkness is at hand.
Trouble and anguish make him afraid.

BILDAD. How often is the candle of the wicked put out!
How often comes their destruction upon them!

ELIPHAZ. They that plow iniquity, reap the same.
By the blast of God they perish;
By the breath of his nostrils are they consumed.

JOB. [*With slowly increasing anger.*] Many times have I
    heard such things;
"The light of the wicked shall be put out.
He shall suck the poison of asps
While the poor are delivered from affliction."
But this I say;
God destroys the perfect with the wicked.
If the scourge slay suddenly
He will laugh at the trial of the innocent.

[*There is the crack of a whip, off. A* TALL SLAVE *comes
through the gate, driving the* COMMON PEOPLE *back before
the slave-borne chair of the* RICH MAN *who is faring forth
upon a journey, surrounded by* FOLLOWERS *and* SERVANTS.
The WOMEN *clasp their* CHILDREN *to their breasts and hide
their faces. The* MEN *bow in fear. One* LITTLE GIRL *who does
not get out of the way quickly enough is thrown down and
trampled but is rescued by* ELIHU. *The* RICH MAN *looks
over the heads of the crowd contemptuously as he is carried
past.* JOB *remains with head unbowed, staring after him*

with a sardonic expression. After a moment he speaks to
ELIHU *who is comforting the* LITTLE GIRL.]

Men groan from out of the city,
Yea, the soul of the wounded cries for justice,
But the earth is given into the hands of evil men
And God covers the eyes of the judges;
If not, where and who is he?

[*Before* ELIHU *can answer* JOB *turns away abruptly and
limps back to his friends.*]

Ye comfort me in vain, seeing in your answers
There still remains only falsehood.
Wherefore do the wicked live, become old,
Wax mighty in wealth and power?
They say unto God, "Depart from us
For we desire not the knowledge of thy ways.
What profit should we have if we pray unto thee?"
Yet their houses are safe from fear.
Neither is the rod of God upon them.

[*A number of* CHILDREN *run in Left carrying toy bows,
arrows and spears. They dodge about the stage, pursuing
some imaginary enemy, then run out Right.*]

ELIPHAZ. The wicked are exalted for a little time
But they are soon brought low.
If their children be multiplied, it is for the sword.

ZOPHAR. Knowest thou not, the triumphing of the wicked is
        short,
And the joy of the ungodly but for a moment?

BILDAD. Because he has stretched out his hand
And strengthened himself against the Almighty,

An evil man walks upon a snare,
He is cast into a net by his own feet.

ZOPHAR. Because he has oppressed and forsaken the poor
His roots shall be dried up beneath.
Above, his branches shall be cut off.
What remains shall be buried in death
And his widow shall not weep.

BILDAD. For this is the portion of a wicked man,
That he shall drink of the wrath of God.

JOB. [*Rebelliously.*] The murderer, rising with the light,
Kills the poor and in the night is a thief.
Does God cast upon him the fury of his wrath?

ELIPHAZ. Yea, his eyes shall see his own destruction.

BILDAD. All darkness is laid up as his treasure.
Though he heap up silver as the dust,
And prepare raiment as the clay,
He may prepare it, but the just shall put it on.
The innocent shall divide his silver.

ZOPHAR. Heaven shall reveal his iniquity,
The earth rise against him.

ELIPHAZ. He will fly away as a dream and not be found.
His remembrance shall perish.

JOB. Why do ye vex my soul
And break me into pieces with words?

BILDAD. If our lips reproach thee it is for thine own good.

ZOPHAR. All that we tell thee we have searched out.

ELIPHAZ. It is so.

JOB. No doubt ye are the people and wisdom will die with
  you,
But I have understanding as well as you.
Listen and give answer!
If a man dies shall he live again?
There is hope of a tree if it be cut down
That it will sprout again.
But man dies and wastes away,
He gives up the ghost, and where is he?
As the cloud is consumed and vanishes,
So he that goes down to the grave shall come no more.

ELIPHAZ. Is there not an appointed time to man upon earth?

BILDAD. His days are determined.
The number of his months are with God
Who has appointed bonds that he cannot pass.

JOB. But one dies in his full strength
Being wholly at ease and quiet.
Another, without food, in the bitterness of his soul.
They lie down alike in the dust
And the worms shall cover them.
Therefore, if I be wicked, why labor I in vain,
Seeing if I wash myself with snow water
And make my hands never so clean,
Still, he will plunge me into the pit?

BILDAD. [*To the other friends.*] Should not this multitude
  of words be answered?

ELIPHAZ. How should a man reason with unprofitable talk,
Or with speeches wherewith he can do no good?

JOB. Your remembrances are like unto ashes,
Your bodies to bodies of clay;
Though I speak, my grief is not assuaged!

[*In despair he turns sharply up Left, crosses to well for a drink. A* PEDDLER *selling loaves of unleavened bread comes out through gate. The* IDLERS *crowd in and jostle* JOB. *One holds a cup of water, then snatches it away. Another does the same. A* SMALL BOY *imitates his limp.* ALL *laugh except* ELIHU *who gives* JOB *water.* JOB'S *next speech is addressed to him, to explain his fumbling for the cup.*]

Mine eye is dim by reason of my sorrow.
Oh, that I were as in months past
In the days when God preserved me,
When his candle shone upon my head,
And my children were about me!
As I went out to the gate through the city
The young men saw me and stood back;
The aged rose and bowed.
When I spoke, all men gave ear.
But now who is there will strike hands with me?
Men whose fathers I would have disdained
To have set with the dogs of my flocks
Hold me in derision!

[*A* SMALL URCHIN *comes up from behind, pulls at his cloak, almost throwing him over. Other* GAMINS *join the game, jerking him this way and that. The* IDLERS *laugh again as he sputters angrily.*]

Children of fools! Spawn of the nameless!
Viler than the dirt!

[*To* ELIHU, *who has driven the imps away and restored his cloak.*]

Now I am their song, yea, I am their byword.
They abhor me and spare not to spit in my face!

[*He turns back toward Right.* ELIHU *goes a few steps, helping him when he stumbles.* JOB *pushes him away harshly.*]

Let me alone! I would not live always.

[*With deep sadness.*]

Since God hath kindled his wrath against me
My soul is weary of this life.

[*Returns to his friends again. Speaks with real humility.*]

Oh, tell me mine iniquities;
Make me know my transgressions
That I may learn why God hath overthrown me!

BILDAD. Thine own mouth utters thine iniquity.

ZOTHAR. Thine own lips condemn thee.

JOB. [*In terrible anger.*] Ye are all forgers of lies! Physicians
   of little value!
I cannot find one wise man among you!

[*During the last speeches* ELIHU *has remained at a little distance, listening. He now moves forward, speaking, at first, with gentleness and modesty, then with slowly increasing authority.*]

ELIHU. I, Elihu, son of Barachel the Buzite, am young,
And ye are very old.
Therefore was I afraid to shew you mine opinion.
I said, "Days should speak,
And multitude of years should teach wisdom."
I waited for your words, while ye searched out what to say;
I gave ear to your reasonings.
There was none of you that convinced Job,
Or that answered his arguments.
Therefore will I open my lips and declare my knowledge.

BILDAD. Shall vain words have no end?
What emboldens thee to answer?

ELIPHAZ. Yea, what knowest thou that we know not?

ZOPHAR. Grey-haired and aged men, much older than thy
    father,
Are in agreement with us.

ELIHU. Great men are not always wise;
Neither do the aged understand judgment.
There is a spirit in man,
And the breath of the Almighty gives him understanding;
I am full of matter and the spirit within me
Constrains me to speak.

JOB. [*Ironically.*] Teach me, and I will hold my tongue.

ELIHU. Thou hast spoken in my hearing, saying,
"I am clean, without transgression;
I am innocent; neither is there iniquity in me.
Yet, God finds occasions against me;
He counts me for his enemy."

BILDAD. Yea, Job has said, "It profits a man nothing
That he should delight himself with God."

JOB. [*Angrily, to* BILDAD.] Ye dig a pit for your friend,
And plead my reproach to magnify yourselves against me!

[*To* ELIHU.]

Is there iniquity in my tongue?
Can not my taste discern perverse things?
Know that God has overthrown me
And encompassed me with his net.
Even today is my complaint bitter!

ELIHU. Many complain of God, but none say,
"Where is God, my maker, who gives songs in the night?
Who teaches us more than the beasts of the earth
And makes us wiser than the fowls of heaven?"

BILDAD. Lo, these are parts of his ways,
But how little a portion is heard of him!
The thunder of his power, who can understand?

ZOPHAR. Yea, God is great and we know him not.
Neither does he give any account of his matters.

JOB. [*Scornfully.*] All this do I know. Is wisdom driven
quite from me?

ELIHU. Suffer me to speak, and then mock on;
If thou sayest, "What advantage will it be to me,
And what profit will I have, if I be cleaned from my sin?"
I answer, "Behold the stars, how high they are!
Is not God in the height of the heavens?"

BILDAD. He is as high as the heaven, what canst thou do?
Deeper than hell, what canst thou know?

JOB. [*Bowing his head in sad agreement.*] With God is a
terrible majesty.

ELIHU. If thou sinnest, what doest thou against him;
Or if thou be righteous, what givest thou him?

BILDAD. He is excellent in power and in judgment.

ELIHU. Why then dost thou strive against him?
Wilt thou condemn the most just?

ZOPHAR. Surely God will not do wickedly.

BILDAD. He will not lay up against a man more than is right.

JOB. I also could speak as ye do,
If my soul were in your soul's stead.
I could shake my head and heap up words against you.
But your reproof, what does it reprove?
Do you think to reprove the words of one who is desperate?

ELIHU. Happy is the man whom God corrects.
Therefore, despise not the chastening of the Almighty.

JOB. Is my strength the strength of stones?
Is my flesh of brass?
God will not suffer me to take my breath,
But fills me with pain.
When I say, "My bed shall comfort me,
My couch shall ease my agony,"
Then does he frighten me with dreams
And terrify me through visions,
So that my soul chooses strangling and death rather than
    life.

ELIHU. In a dream, in a vision of the night,
When deep sleep falls upon men,
God speaks once, yea, twice, yet man understands him not.
To remove man from his evil and keep his soul from the pit,
He is chastened with pain upon his bed.
His flesh is consumed away that it cannot be seen.
His bones that were not seen stick out.

ZOPHAR. His soul draws near unto the grave,
His life to the Destroyer.

JOB. [*Despairingly.*] Where then is my hope? Who shall
    see it?

ELIHU. Is not thy fear of God thy confidence
And thy righteous ways thy hope?

God is mighty and despises not any ;
His eyes are upon the ways of man,
And he sees all his goings. If any say,
"I have sinned and perverted that which was right,
Pardon thou my transgressions and take away mine
    iniquity !"
He will deliver his soul from the pit
And his life shall see light.

ELIPHAZ. His flesh shall be fresher than a child's,
He shall return to the days of his youth.

ZOPHAR. All these things God works often time with man !

ELIHU. He opens men's ears to discipline
And commands that they return from iniquity.
If they obey and serve him
They shall spend their days in prosperity
And their years in pleasures.
Even so would he remove thee out of the strait
Into a broad place where there is no straitness.

ELIPHAZ. God shall fill thy mouth with laughing.

BILDAD. Thou shalt forget thy misery
Or remember it as waters that pass away.

ELIHU. Therefore acquaint thyself now with him and be at
    peace.
For when he gives quietness, who can make trouble?
Surely it is meet to say unto God,
"I have borne chastisement,
That which I see not, teach thou me ;
If I have done iniquity, I will do it no more."

JOB. It is so of a truth,
But oh, that I knew where I might find him !

I go forward, but he is not there,
And backward, but I cannot perceive him.

ZOPHAR. [*Shocked.*] Dost thou hope by thy searchings to
  find out God?

ELIHU. Concerning the Almighty, we cannot find him out.
When he hides his face, who can behold him?

JOB. [*Despairingly.*] Where, then, shall wisdom be found?
Where is the place of understanding?
Seeing it is hid from the eyes of the living
And kept close from the fowls of the air?

ELIHU. God understands the way thereof.
And he knows the place thereof,
For he looks to the ends of the earth,
And sees under the whole heaven.

JOB. Oh, that one might plead for a man with God
As a man pleads for his neighbor!
But he is not a man, as I am,
That we should talk together.
If I speak of strength, lo, he is strong;
And if I pray for justice, who shall set me a time to plead?

BILDAD. If God will not withdraw his anger,
The proud helpers do stoop under him.

JOB. How much less shall I answer him,
And choose out my words to reason with him?
For terrors are turned upon me,
They pursue my soul as the wind.
Oh, let him take his rod away from me,
And let not his anger terrify me;
Then would I speak, and not fear him!

[*Two* STREET MUSICIANS *and a* JUGGLER *come from Right and cross to Left where they entice the crowd to follow them through the gates into the city.* JOB *is left alone with* ELIHU *and his friends.*]

ELIHU. Behold, I am according to thy wish in God's stead;
I also am formed out of the clay,
The spirit of God has made me,
And the breath of the Almighty has given me life.
My terror shall not make thee afraid.
Therefore suffer me that I speak on God's behalf.

JOB. Dost thou dare to speak for God?
Surely he will reprove thee!
What ye know, the same do I know also.
I am not inferior to you.

ELIHU. Who is like Job? He drinks up scorning like water!
[*To* JOB.]
In this thou art not just.
I will answer thee, that God is greater than man.

JOB. Is my complaint to man? I would reason with God!

BILDAD. [*Terrified.*] If a man speak thus, surely he shall be
    swallowed up!

JOB. I would seek unto God, and unto God would I commit
    my cause.
I know that I shall be justified.

ELIHU. How should a man be justified with God?
If he contend with him,
He cannot answer him one of a thousand!
He is wise in heart, and mighty in strength.
Who has hardened himself against him and has prospered?

JOB. I have ordered my case;
When he has tried me, I shall come forth pure gold,
For my witness is in heaven and my record is on high.

ELIHU. [*Sternly.*] Is it fit to say to a king, "Thou art
    wicked"?
And to princes, "Ye are ungodly"?
How much less to him that accepts not the persons of
    princes!

JOB. [*Stubbornly.*] He breaks me with tempests
And multiplies my wounds without cause,
Therefore will I not restrain my mouth.
I will speak in the anguish of my spirit;
I will complain in the bitterness of my soul!
My desire is that the Almighty should answer me.

ZOPHAR. Beware lest God cast the fury of his wrath upon
    you!

JOB. Let come on me, what will!
Though he slay me, yet will I trust him.
But I will maintain my own ways before him.

BILDAD. Call, then, if there be any that answer thee!

JOB. [*Very simply.*] Oh Lord, my God,
Withdraw thy rod from me
And let not thy dread make me afraid;
Then call thou, and I will answer,
Or let me speak and answer thou me.

[*An instant's pause while he looks toward heaven.*]

Oh, God, thou art become cruel to me!
Thou hast fashioned me out of the clay,

Thou hast granted me life and favor,
Is it good that thou shouldst despise the works of thine
    hands
And shine upon the counsel of the wicked?

ELIHU. He hath added rebellion unto his other sins!

[*Lights begin to dim very slowly.*]

JOB. Thou knowest I am not wicked.
Did I not weep for him that was in trouble?
Was not my soul grieved for the poor?
I was eyes to the blind, and feet to the lame,
Father to the fatherless,
And blessed by him about to perish.
Yet when I looked for good, evil came upon me.
When I waited for light, there came darkness.

[JOB'S WIFE *comes in from gate, moves toward him, frightened by the gathering gloom.*]

Are not my days few?
They are passing away as the swift ships,
As the eagle that hastens to his prey.
Why dost thou not pardon my transgressions
And take away mine iniquities
That I may take comfort a little
Before I go whence I shall not return?

[*His* WIFE *sinks down, sobbing, head in hands.*]

Soon I shall sleep in the dust.
Thou shalt seek me in the morning, and I shall not be.
Therefore, show me, Oh Lord, why thou contendest with
    me,
For I am full of confusion.

[*Again he waits, eyes uplifted, then speaks with a return of his old anger and despair.*]

I cry out of wrong, but I am not heard!
I cry aloud, but there is no justice!
Oh, earth, cover not thou my blood,
And let my cry have no place!

[*As he stands, hands upraised, in a gesture of magnificent protest, there is a rumble of thunder. Lightning flashes. The* INHABITANTS *of the village crowd out from the city gates, the* SHEPHERDS *and* WORKERS *run in from Left and Right.* ALL *are terrified with the exception of* ELIHU, *who speaks with exaltation.*]

ELIHU. Behold, God thunders marvelously with his voice! The pillars of heaven tremble and are astonished at his reproof!

[*A Light grows off Right, not very strong, still far away.* ALL *look and then bow down. Some prostrate themselves upon the ground. Only* ELIHU *and* JOB *remain standing so that the light is at first upon them, with* JOB *receiving the larger share.*]

VOICE. Who is this that darkens counsel
By words without knowledge?

JOB. [*To* ELIHU.] My heart trembles and is moved out of its place.

[*Toward the light.*]

Have pity upon me, oh thou Preserver of Men!

VOICE. Art thou the first man that was born?
Or wast thou made before the hills?
Hast thou heard the secret of God,

In whose hand is the soul of every living thing,
And the breath of all mankind?

ELIHU. [*Chanting reverently.*] Who discovers deep things
    out of darkness,
And brings out to light the shadow of death.

VOICE. Where wast thou when I laid the foundations of the
    earth?
Declare, if thou hast understanding,
Who laid the cornerstone thereof,
And fixed the measurements,
When the morning stars sang together
And all the Heavenly Beings shouted for joy?
Who shut up the sea with doors when it brake forth
And said, "Thus far shalt thou come, but no farther,
Here shalt thy proud waves be stayed?"

ELIHU. [*Chanting.*] He hath compassed the waters with
    bounds,
Until the day and night come to an end.

VOICE. Hast thou ever commanded the morning,
Or caused the dawn to know its place?
Hast thou entered into the depths of the sea,
Or have the gates of death been opened unto thee?
Canst thou bind the sweet influences of Pleiades,
Or loose the bands of Orion?

ELIHU. Hearken, hearken, oh Job:
Consider the wondrous works of thy God.
Of him who is perfect in knowledge!

VOICE. Shall he who contends with the Almighty instruct him
Who has put wisdom in the inward parts,
Who has given understanding to the heart?

He that reproves God, let him answer!

JOB. Oh Lord, it is so.
I have spoken without comprehension
Of things too wonderful for me to know.

VOICE. Shall mortal man be more just than God?
Shall a man be more pure than his Maker?

JOB. Behold, I am nothing!
I abhor myself, and repent in dust and ashes!

VOICE. Deck thyself now with honor and majesty.
Look upon everyone that is proud; abase him,
And tread down the wicked where they stand;
Then will I confess that thine own hand can save thee,
For the fear of the Lord is wisdom
And to depart from evil is understanding.

ELIHU. [*Chanting.*] Dominion and fear are with him,
He maketh peace in his high places.

ALL. [*Chanting.*] He maketh sore and he bindeth up,
He woundeth and his hands make whole.

JOB. I have heard of thee by the hearing of the ear:
But now mine eye seeth.
Oh, that my words were graven in the rock forever,
I know that my redeemer liveth!
After this, my body, is destroyed,
Then, without flesh, shall I see God!

[*Light grows brighter and spreads to take in* ELIPHAZ,
BILDAD *and* ZOPHAR.]

VOICE. My servant Job hath spoken of me the thing which is
right.

But thou, Eliphaz, the Temanite,
My wrath is kindled against thee, and against thy two
    friends,
Therefore, take unto you now seven bullocks and seven
    rams.
Offer up for yourselves a burnt offering,
Lest I deal with thee according to thy folly.

ELIPHAZ, BILDAD, ZOPHAR. [*Prostrating themselves.*] Thus
    will we do, oh Lord!

VOICE. My servant Job shall pray for you.
His prayers will I accept.
His latter end shall be more blessed than his beginning,
With sons and with daughters,
With camel and oxen and sheep beyond counting.
He shall see his sons and his sons' sons,
Even unto the fourth generation.
He shall die old and full of days.

ELIHU. The righteous shall be glad in the Lord
And shall trust him!
And all of the upright in heart shall rejoice!

[*The off-stage light has grown in intensity, the stage lights
also come up. The* VILLAGERS *rise, exultant and happy.*]

JOB. Oh, Lord, my God, I cried unto thee
And thou hast healed me.
Thou hast brought up my soul from the grave;
Thou hast kept me alive
That I should not go down to the pit.
Sing unto the Lord and give thanks.
Give thanks at the remembrance of his holiness!

VOICE. For whatever is under the whole heavens is mine.

JOB AND ELIHU. Thine is the power and the glory!

ALL. Oh, clap your hands, all ye people!
Shout unto God with the voice of triumph.
Sing praises to God, sing praises!
Sing praises unto God, our King!
Sing praises!

[*The light on the stage is now brilliant, flooding the whole scene as* JOB *and the* PEOPLE *rejoice.*]

THE CURTAIN FALLS

ALBUQUERQUE TEN MINUTES

A One-Act Comedy

BY

FLORENCE RYERSON

CHARACTERS

TOMAS
MEETA
MRS. HOSKINS
CANDICE LYNN
BILL BAILEY

TIME

The present.

SCENE

A room in the station at Albuquerque, New Mexico.

ALBUQUERQUE TEN MINUTES

The Santa Fe station in Albuquerque rambles over a good deal of territory, with lunch and waiting rooms, magazine and news stands, telephone booths and curio shops. This is one of the smaller rooms, shallow, with a single bench and a large stone jar, intended as a receptacle for trash. Its principal features, unless you count the Indians, TOMAS *and* MEETA, *are a telephone booth at Left and an arched entrance raked at an angle upper Right. A walk leads to this entrance, but the view beyond is cut off by shrubbery.*

It is morning of a pleasant Spring day. The two INDIANS, *both fairly young, are seated on a blanket half inside, half outside the archway. Their backs are turned toward the room, but subsequent actions show they are stolid and poker-faced.* TOMAS *is bare-footed.*

At Rise: MRS. HOSKINS *a middle-aged tourist, is fussily selecting a beadwork belt.*

MRS. HOSKINS. I'll take this one—no—*that*. No—wait—that's pink, isn't it? My sister doesn't like pink. But the beadwork's much prettier. Can't you show me something in that beadwork but this color—oh, dear, I suppose you don't understand English, or do you?

TOMAS. One dollyar.

MEETA. [*Nodding her head affirmatively.*] Ugh!

MRS. HOSKINS. No, I didn't ask the price. I said—oh, never mind! I see just what I want over there—

[*Starts rapidly off, colliding with* CANDICE LYNN *as she comes in from the Right.* CANDICE *is concealing considerable beauty under the wide brim of her hat and behind dark glasses of the "pixie" type.* MRS. HOSKINS *knocks both askew.* CANDICE *straightens them with difficulty since she is carrying magazines and a bag of salted nuts in addition to her handbag.*]

MRS. HOSKINS. Oh, I'm dreadfully sorry, but it's so difficult when they only give you ten minutes and every second you're expecting to hear the conductor yell "All aboard!"—and they *will* make everything the most hideous pink— [*A sudden yell which makes* CANDICE *jump.*] Wait a minute! [*To* CANDICE *again.*] That woman's grabbing my belt! [*As she charges off Left.*] That's mine! I want it!

[CANDICE *straightens her hat and glasses, again knocked crooked by* MRS. HOSKINS, *then picks up the pink belt.*]

TOMAS. Two dollyar.

MEETA. [*Same business.*] Ugh!

CANDICE. I didn't ask the price. I was just looking— Oh, good grief!

[*This, as she apparently sees someone out of scene, toward the Left. She pulls her hat down over her face, then scuttles into the room where she stands looking at a poster, her back to the arch.* BILL BAILEY *comes in from Left. He is young, tall, good-looking, suggests the wide open spaces in his dress, but when he speaks his words are clipped and business-like.*]

BILL. Hello, Chief, did you see a girl—

TOMAS. [*Holding up same pink belt.*] T'ree dollyar.

MEETA. Ugh!

BILL. No! No! I asked if you saw a girl—

MRS. HOSKINS. [*Coming in excitedly from Right.*] Excuse me, but I've just heard that Candice Lynn's on board the train. Have you seen her anywhere?

BILL. [*Drawling.*] Well, now, Ma'am, I can't say as I have, and I can't say as I haven't. If you could tell me what she looks like—

MRS. HOSKINS. [*Shocked.*] Why, she looks like—Candice Lynn. She *is* Candice Lynn, you know—from the New York stage.

BILL. [*Helpfully.*] We got a Las Vegas stage—and one from Santa Fe, but about a stage from New York—you'd have to ask around.

MRS. HOSKINS. That's not what I mean! Oh, dear! She's one of my favorite actresses and I don't want to— [*Sees someone out of scene, hurries out.*] Porter! Have *you* seen Candice Lynn?

[*As her voice dies away* BILL *steps into the room, speaks without drawl.*]

BILL. Hello, Candy.

CANDICE. [*Swinging around with slightly overdone surprise.*] Why, Bill Bailey! I can't believe my eyes! What are you doing here? [*Without giving him a chance to answer.*] How are you? You're looking well! Wonderful! I didn't see you on the train, or are you here shooting a picture? Of course! You're shooting a picture!

BILL. I've just finished a picture.

CANDICE. That's fine. [*Moving toward exit.*] I'd love to stop and talk but they only give us ten minutes—

BILL. You've got longer than that. The train's staying over-time.

CANDICE. The Chief never stays overtime.

BILL. She's doing it today. There's some trouble about ice. That porter just told me.

CANDICE. I still don't believe it.

BILL. Would I lie to you?

CANDICE. Like a shot. [*Suddenly giggles.*] Remember that whopper you told me in Boston?

BILL. About the plane being grounded by fog?

CANDICE. Mm.

BILL. It worked, didn't it!

CANDICE. It kept me in Boston overnight, if that's what you mean.

BILL. That's what I mean. [*Grins.*] You didn't seem to mind at the time.

CANDICE. But it doesn't make for confidence. [*To* TOMAS.] Have you heard when the train is leaving?

TOMAS. [*Holding up two belts.*] Four dollyar.

MEETA. Ugh.

CANDICE. No, I asked about the train—the *train!* [*Calls off Right.*] Porter—do you know?

PORTER'S VOICE. Not leavin' fo' ten-fifteen minutes, Miss. They's some trouble about ice.

CANDICE. [*Turns back, meets* BILL's *triumphant grin.*] You probably stole it. I wouldn't put it past you.

BILL. Cross my heart, lady!

CANDICE. I never knew you had one.

MRS. HOSKINS. [*Pops in breathlessly.*] Excuse me, but I'm looking for Miss Candice Lynn—

CANDICE. [*Promptly, in a sticky voice.*] You don't mean Miss *Lynn* the *stage* actress?

MRS. HOSKINS. Yes, that one. They say she's somewhere on the train.

CANDICE. Oh, goody! I'm just crazy to see her! [*Simpering.*] Everybody says we look alike.

MRS. HOSKINS. Well, I did think for a minute—but of course you're much older. [*She trots out.*]

CANDICE. [*Indignantly—to* BILL.] Older than what?

MRS. HOSKINS. [*Popping back in.*] They say Bill Bailey's around somewhere, too, but I don't go for Westerns. [*She pops out again.*]

BILL. [*Comfortingly.*] She didn't recognize me, either.

CANDICE. She wouldn't be likely to—without your horse. By the way, how is he? Never mind answering, I'm sure he's all right or you wouldn't be here.

BILL. Now, Candy—

CANDICE. You and that horse! You could leave me practically dying—

BILL. You only had the hives—

CANDICE. It might have struck in. [*Finishing earlier speech.*] Practically dying—to go sit by that brute and hold his hoof.

BILL. I told you I couldn't trust that vet.

CANDICE. [*In a pretty rage.*] The first girl in history to be stood up for a horse!

BILL. That wasn't the real reason you were so mad at me.

CANDICE. You think not?

BILL. It was because I wouldn't lie down and let you walk on me.

CANDICE. You let your horse do it. I saw it in that picture— *Saddle Pals.*

BILL. My horse doesn't trample on me.

CANDICE. And I suppose I would have.

BILL. With both feet. Hard.

CANDICE. Well, I must say— [*Breaks off.*] You know, I'd forgotten how infuriating you could be. It's heavenly luck we never married. I've been saved years of wretchedness.

BILL. You don't really believe that.

CANDICE. [*Putting her things down on bench with a bump.*] Of course I believe it.

BILL. Then it shows how little you know yourself. But then you never did.

CANDICE. That's ridiculous—

BILL. You don't even know why we broke things off.

CANDICE. That's easy. We agreed marriage wouldn't work.

Not for us. I was in New York while you were in the West—
the width of the continent apart—

BILL. It didn't have to be that way—

CANDICE. Of course it didn't. But you chose to be stubborn—

BILL. No stubborner than you.

CANDICE. The situation was quite different. I was already
established in a profession.

BILL. So was I.

CANDICE. You can scarcely compare the two. You could just
as easily have lived in New York.

BILL. And sat around night clubs waiting for you to finish
your performance?

CANDICE. There was no need for you to sit. You could have
had a Broadway part just by lifting your finger.

BILL. New York's no place to raise a family.

CANDICE. We could have lived in Nyack or Westchester—

BILL. [*Cutting in.*] —or Brooklyn.

CANDICE. Don't try to be funny. [*With increasing indigna-
tion.*] Really! The idea of your expecting me to give up
my work to go splashing around in Hollywood swimming
pools—

BILL. There's no law forcing you to splash.

CANDICE. I was speaking figuratively. And speaking of fig-
ures, whatever became of that blonde?

BILL. Which blonde?

CANDICE. The one who played that revolting heroine in *Sundown Bleach*.

BILL. *Sundown Beach*.

CANDICE. Just a slip of the tongue.

BILL. She's married. There was never anything in that rumor, but I'm glad you're still jealous.

CANDICE. Jealous? How absurd! I'm nothing of the kind. [*The telephone rings.*] There's the telephone.

BILL. So I notice.

[*Telephone rings.*]

CANDICE. Don't you think we ought to answer?

BILL. Why?

[*Telephone rings.*]

CANDICE. We can't just ignore it.

BILL. Why?

[*Telephone rings.*]

CANDICE. Will you stop saying "Why?"! [*Telephone rings.*] Oh! I can't stand it!

BILL. O.K. [*Into telephone.*] Hello!—Not that I know of—

CANDICE. What does it want?

BILL. Someone named "Myrtle."

CANDICE. Perhaps it's— [*To* MEETA.] Are you Myrtle?

TOMAS. [*Hopefully holding up three belts.*] Fi' dollyars.

MEETA. Ugh.

CANDICE. [*To* BILL.] Not Myrtle.

BILL. [*Into telephone.*] You'd better call later. [*Hangs up.*]

CANDICE. [*Who has been staring at* MEETA.] Do you suppose she ever says anything but "Ugh"?

BILL. She doesn't need to. Her husband does the talking for the family.

CANDICE. That would exactly suit you. A wife who said "Ugh"—[*A bob of the head in imitation of* MEETA.]—whenever you made a statement.

BILL. It might have its advantages.

CANDICE. [*Still looking at the stolid couple.*] I wonder how they work it out? I mean, they look happy—

BILL. If you call that looking.

CANDICE. Well, anyway, *satisfied*. I wonder how they solve their problems?

BILL. They don't have any problems. You can bet he started right. When he decided he wanted her, he just grabbed her by the hair—

CANDICE. It isn't long enough.

BILL. By the nape of her neck, then, and dragged her off to his cave.

CANDICE. Which you wanted to do with me.

BILL. Which I *should* have done with you.

CANDICE. D'you know, you were born out of your time. You

would have fitted nicely into the Stone Age. You and your horse.

BILL. If I'd had any brains I'd have grabbed you up and run off with you two years ago. Then today you'd be—

CANDICE. [*Cutting in.*] Sitting on a blanket, grunting "Ugh."

BILL. And looking satisfied.

CANDICE. I *am* satisfied, thank you.

BILL. You don't look it.

CANDICE. If you don't like my looks— [*Breaks off.*] Oh dear—there we go again!

BILL. Like old times—huh?

CANDICE. Exactly.

BILL. [*Reminiscently.*] We sure staged some rare battles.

CANDICE. Every time we met.

BILL. Not *every* time— [*She looks at him.*] 'Member that week I did personal appearances in Minneapolis?

CANDICE. And I was playing St. Paul!

BILL. I've always wondered what our performances looked like from the front.

CANDICE. I've never wanted to know.

BILL. We were practically delirious.

CANDICE. Floating on bubbles— [*A catch of her breath.*] Oh, why couldn't it have stayed that way always?

BILL. It can't always be Spring.

CANDICE. No— [*Softly.*] Remember the hyacinths?

BILL. And the dogwood—

CANDICE. Pink and white—

BILL. That time we went rowing on the river—

CANDICE. And you bought me a peppermint lollypop!

BILL. Your lips were sticky when I kissed you—

CANDICE. Don't!

BILL. Still hurts—doesn't it?

CANDICE. Not a bit.

BILL. Liar! [*Softly.*] It's not too late.

CANDICE. Yes, it is—

BILL. We're still young and healthy.

CANDICE. You can't warm over something that's gone cold.

BILL. It's never gone cold—not for me—

CANDICE. [*Turns away quickly.*] Please—

BILL. —Nor for you, either.

CANDICE. It has! It has!

BILL. Then why are you crying?

CANDICE. I'm not crying—I'm laughing. At us. Two hard-boiled moderns, going sentimental over dogwood and lolly-pops.

BILL. If you're not crying why are your cheeks wet? [*She puts her hands up quickly to her cheeks, he pulls them down again.*] Darling, why don't you give in? Admit you've missed me as much as I've missed you?

CANDICE. Because I'm not—I mean I haven't. [*Very fast.*] My life suits me perfectly—I'm happy the way I am.

BILL. Then why are you heading West?

CANDICE. For a vacation. Can't a girl take a vacation?

BILL. In Hollywood?

CANDICE. I've friends out there—

BILL. Studio friends.

CANDICE. Naturally.

BILL. But you're just going for a vacation?

CANDICE. What else would I be going for?

[*Telephone rings.*]

BILL. Damn! [*Picks up telephone.*] Hello. Yes—no—

CANDICE. Myrtle again?

BILL. [*Nods.*] It seems Gussie wants her.

MRS. HOSKINS. [*Swoops in, a newspaper under her arm.*] Wait! Don't hang up! That's for me! I put in a call and they switched it in here. [*Into telephone.*] Hello! Hello! That you, Gussie? This is Myrtle—yes—in Albuquerque. [*To* CANDICE *and* BILL.] Just go right on talking, I won't be a minute. [*Into telephone.*] No, nothing's happened, but listen! Candice Lynn is aboard our train—mm—she's locked into her drawing-room but she's got to come out sometime. I thought you might drive up and get on at Pasadena—mm—if you stood outside her door you could get her autograph. [*To the* OTHERS, *indicating telephone.*] She's nabbed just about everybody but Lynn and the Pope—and she's written to him. [*Into telephone again.*] You can't? Oh, well, you can probably catch her at the studio—mm—I understand she's coming out to do a picture.

BILL. How's that?

MRS. HOSKINS. It's here in the paper. [*Into telephone again.*] Can't talk any more—no time.

BILL. [*Grabbing* CANDICE, *who is trying to slip out.*] You stay here!

MRS. HOSKINS. [*Into telephone at same time.*] 'Bye, now! Be seeing you t'morrow! [*Hangs up, starts for arch, stops.*] If you'd like to read about it— [*Pushes paper folded at drama page into* BILL's *hand.*] You're welcome. [*She trots out.*]

[BILL *looks from paper to* CANDICE.]

CANDICE. All right! I give in! I'm going to do a picture.

BILL. Why didn't you tell me?

CANDICE. If you can't guess why—

BILL. Honey—

CANDICE. I wanted you to give in first.

BILL. [*Grinning.*] I did.

CANDICE. Did what?

BILL. Give in. I'm on my way East to do a play in New York.

CANDICE. Oh, *no!*

BILL. Yes!

[*They look at each other, begin to laugh.*]

CANDICE. It's too marvelous!

BILL. Life wasn't worth living without you—

CANDICE. I know—

BILL. I couldn't stand it any longer—

CANDICE. Neither could I!

BILL. So I said, "To hell with Hollywood" and jumped into my car—

CANDICE. I said, "Goodbye, Broadway" and took the train— [*They are holding onto each other now, laughing helplessly.*] Oh, dear! Oh, dear! This ought to be a lesson to us!

BILL. We can't live apart.

CANDICE. We've got to be together.

BILL. No matter what!

CANDICE. No matter what! [*As he starts Right.*] Where are you going?

BILL. To get your things off the train.

CANDICE. Wait!

BILL. No time to wait! We'll throw 'em in my car—find a minister—then head East—

CANDICE. Oh, we will!

BILL. Make the trip our honeymoon.

CANDICE. And what about my picture!

BILL. Wire the studio and call it off.

CANDICE. Why not wire your producer to call off your play?

BILL. Because I've already signed.

CANDICE. So have I. [*He stares, stricken.*] A long-term contract—if I photograph well.

BILL. [*Hopefully.*] Maybe you won't.

CANDICE. Thank you so much.

BILL. I don't mean you're not beautiful—

CANDICE. Just a little too old.

BILL. Candy!

CANDICE. Or not blonde enough.

BILL. Stop it! Stop it!

CANDICE. I'm sorry.

BILL. So am I. [*An instant's pause while they look at each other.*] What are we going to do?

CANDICE. [*Hopeful in her turn.*] Perhaps your play will only run a few nights.

BILL. My producer says it will run for years.

CANDICE. He would.

BILL. Are you going to give it the kiss of death before we start rehearsals?

CANDICE. I was only trying to figure some way we could be together.

BILL. Try figuring from *your* end.

[*From now on they keep interrupting each other's speeches.*]

CANDICE. By that I suppose you mean—

BILL. It's a woman's place to follow her husband.

CANDICE. What husband?

BILL. Now, see here—

CANDICE. I haven't any husband—

MRS. HOSKINS. [*Popping her head in.*] Train leaves in two minutes! [*Pops out.*]

CANDICE. Saved!

BILL. You can't leave like this.

CANDICE. Just watch me!

[*Starts out, remembers her things, runs back Left. Voices in distance are calling,* "All on train!" "Train leaving!" "One minute!" *etc.*]

TOMAS. [*To* BILL, *holding out four belts in a last appeal.*] Six dollyars!

MEETA. Ugh!

BILL. [*Suddenly.*] Say that again!

TOMAS. Six dollyars.

MEETA. Ugh!

CANDICE. [*Comes back from Left, tries to push past* BILL *who is blocking the arch.*] Will you kindly let me pass?

BILL. Not on your life!

CANDICE. What? [*As he takes her arm.*] What are you doing?

BILL. What I should have done two years ago!

CANDICE. You'll make me lose my train—

BILL. You betcha! Hey, Red Cap!

VOICE. [*Off.*] Yes, sir!

BILL. Get the bags out of drawing-room number— [*To* CANDICE.] What number?

CANDICE. I won't tell you.

BILL. Want to be dragged by the hair?

CANDICE. No! Stop!

BILL. The papers would love it.

CANDICE. O—Oh!

BILL. [*Taking a firm grip.*] Make up your mind.

CANDICE. [*Giving in.*] Car 91—B.

BILL. [*Calling out of scene.*] 91-B. And put them in that Lincoln!

CANDICE. The studio will sue me for a million.

BILL. I'll pay it! [*To* TOMAS.] Here—I'll take those. All of 'em! [*Crams money into his hand, takes the belts, loops them around* CANDICE'S *neck like a halter.*] Vamoose!

CANDICE. Bill! Stop it! Let me go! Stop it!

BILL. Come on, Squaw!

[*He pulls her out,* BOTH *laughing.*]

CONDUCTOR. [*Off stage.*] All aboard! All aboard!

[*Sounds of train leaving; not too loud since the Chief is a streamliner. The* INDIANS *hold their pose for a moment, then* TOMAS *throws off his blanket, stretches his arms.*]

TOMAS. Well, that's that!

MEETA. [*Also discarding her blanket.*] Yeah. [*Reaches over casually, takes money from him, tucks it down the front of her dress.*] Time we were getting home.

TOMAS. [*One anxious eye on her.*] I kind of thought I'd stay down t'night—shoot a little pool.

MEETA. Think again, Big Boy! [*Starts loading him down with the blankets, pots, beadwork, etc.*] Here, take these.

TOMAS. [*Resignedly.*] Ugh!

MEETA. I managed to get a sitter for the papoose. You're taking me to that new hot-spot down the road—

TOMAS. Ugh!

MEETA. [*Loading a final pot on top of the others.*] And what's more—you're going to wear shoes.

[*Picks up a concealed pair of very fancy brown and white sport shoes—holds them out.*]

TOMAS. Ugh. [*Meekly takes shoes—follows her out.*]

CURTAIN

GOING! GOING! GONE!

A One-Act Comedy

BY

FLORENCE RYERSON

CHARACTERS

PARKER GORDON

ELIZABETH GORDON (BITS)

LINDA GORDON (LINNY)

GAYLORD GORDON (GAY)

JOE HAMISH

TIME

The Present.

SCENE

Living room-dining room of the Gordon house in Lake-town.

GOING! GOING! GONE!

The main room of the Gordon house has been planned for modern living, with a fireplace upper Center, hall entrance at Right, door to kitchen and service quarters upper Left. French windows, raked to show a bit of garden and driveway, occupy most of the Left wall.

A folding dining-table is down Left at first, but is later moved upstage. Two chairs and a reading-lamp are at Right of fireplace. A small desk with telephone, down Right, a mirror on the wall above it. The furniture is a pleasant combination of modern and period, the color scheme warmly cheerful.

At rise, the Gordon family is finishing breakfast. GAY GORDON *is seated on the Left, his face concealed by an open newspaper.* LINNY, *a pretty woman in her late thirties, is across from him.* BITS, *thirteen, all knees and elbows, is in the upstage chair. She is studying a fashion magazine.* PARKER, *fifteen, is seated back to the audience. He has twisted himself across the table in order to read a travel advertisement on the reverse side of his father's newspaper.*

PARKER. Gosh! Can you feature that? You can fly clean to Paramaribo in thirteen hours! You can fly to *Zanzibar* in thirty!

BITS. [*Very disdainful.*] Who wants to? [*Displaying her magazine.*] Look, Momps, there's a strapless, backless formal like the one I want.

LINNY. Goodness, it doesn't hide much!

PARKER. What's she got to hide?

BITS. That gag's got whiskers.

LINNY. [*Rises, goes up to get tray.*] "Whiskers"! That reminds me!—Gay, I'm going to need some money for the cleaners.

GAY. [*Comes out from behind his newspaper. He is a good-looking, humorous man of forty-two or three.*] You're welcome. But why should whiskers remind you—

BITS. They're the Lincoln cleaners, Dad.

LINNY. It's perfectly simple.

GAY. Perfectly. [*Brings out check from his bill fold.*] Here's your house money.

LINNY. [*Takes check, kisses him.*] Thank you, darling. You didn't need to give it to me so early.

GAY. Early? It's the fifteenth.

LINNY. [*Starts to pile dishes on tray.*] Oh, no. It's the thirteenth.

PARKER. Fifteenth, Mom—

LINNY. I don't think so.

GAY. This newspaper does.

LINNY. Then it must be an old paper. I looked at my calendar only this morning.

GAY. If you will insist on using a last year's calendar—

BITS. Momps likes the quotations, "A thought for every day."

LINNY. And I'm *used* to it.

PARKER. I don't see how you work it, Momps.

LINNY. It's perfectly simple. I just look at my calendar and add one. I mean, if today is the first then I know its the second and Monday is Tuesday—unless it's Leap Year.

GAY. Clear as crystal!

LINNY. It is to me. For instance, today is Friday—

BITS. It's Saturday.

LINNY. Oh, no!

PARKER. Yes, Saturday.

GAY. The fifteenth of June.

LINNY. [*Promptly.*] Then you ought to be ashamed of yourself.

GAY. *I* should!

LINNY. Yes, *you*. Doesn't the fifteenth of June mean anything to you?

GAY. You bet it does. Income tax.

LINNY. Gaylord Gordon!

GAY. Should it mean something else?

LINNY. You seemed to think it did, once. Eighteen years ago.

GAY. Eighteen years—let me see. Wasn't that the year I broke my leg?

BITS. My goodness, Daddy—

PARKER. It was the year you married Momps!

GAY. [*Snapping his fingers.*] I had a feeling there was something!

LINNY. [*Coldly.*] Like breaking your leg!

[*Front doorbell buzzes.*]

BITS. That's the mailman. I'll go.

LINNY. Wait, Bits! I want to speak with him. [*Pushes tray into* GAY'S *hands.*] You might carry this out—and don't forget to feed the chickens. [*Exits into hall.*]

PARKER. [*As they finish clearing table.*] Gosh, Dad, you pulled a boner, forgetting your anniversary.

GAY. [*Chuckling.*] Not me!

PARKER. Not—?

GAY. Pretty good act, huh? I wanted to throw your mother off the scent because I'm planning to surprise her.

PARKER. With what?

GAY. With a—sh!

[*Moves toward kitchen as* BITS *re-enters from hall.*]

BITS. Nothing for you, Dad, except some ads.

GAY. Well, they're better than bills.

[*Goes off, followed by* PARKER *who carries the toaster and coffee pot.*]

BITS. [*Softly.*] It's all right, Momps. They're gone.

LINNY. [*Enters, opening letter.*] I don't want your father to see this—

BITS. What is it?

LINNY. Dividend on that stock Gramma left me. I've been waiting for it to come before I bought his anniversary present.

BITS. What're you getting him?

LINNY. A perfectly beautiful love-seat.

BITS. You don't mean that thing in the shop up the street!

LINNY. Mm—MacGregor's Antiques.

BITS. But Momps, the stuffing's coming out. The legs are wobbly! It must be a thousand years old!

LINNY. [*Dreamily.*] Yes. It's lovely. Just like a seat Gramma had in her parlor. Your father and I did our canoodling on it.

BITS. What's canoodling?

LINNY. [*Snapping out of her dream.*] What's—? Oh, it's studying for examinations, dear. As soon as I get rid of your father I'll telephone Mr. MacGregor to deliver the seat. He's crazy about it.

BITS. Mr. MacGregor is?

LINNY. Your father.

BITS. Why, no, he isn't Momps. Don't you remember what he said when he passed the window last week—

LINNY. [*Too quickly.*] He didn't say anything of the kind. And anyway, he'll love it when he gets used to it.

BITS. [*Doubtfully.*] He's never got used to those boudoir curtains you gave him last Christmas.

LINNY. This is different. I'm paying cash.

BITS. [*Surprised.*] You are!

LINNY. [*Crossing Left.*] This stock dividend gives me just enough. [*Folds dining-table, carries it upstage with* BITS' *assistance.*] Mr. MacGregor was asking a hundred but I got him down to eighty-five.

BITS. Eighty-five *dollars?*

LINNY. I've been saving it out of the house money; feeding your father round steak instead of sirloin, margarine instead of butter.

BITS. But Daddy doesn't eat margarine.

LINNY. He just thinks he doesn't. [*Puts bowl of flowers on table.*] Oh, dear! I've so much to *do!* A fancy dinner to get, and I must call Mr. MacGregor— [*A glance out French windows.*] There goes Sam Seward down his drive— Please catch him for me, dear!

BITS. [*At windows.*] Mr. Seward! Yoo—oo! Mr. Seward! Mom wants to speak to you!

LINNY. [*Finishes with table and goes to window.*] I'm going to ask him to let me put the seat in his garage until after dinner tonight. Then we'll surprise your father.

BITS. [*Following her mother off.*] He'll be surprised, all right.

GAY. [*Enters from kitchen with* PARKER.] I've been reading about a new kind of chicken-pen wired for television—

PARKER. "It makes the hens set"—I know that one! [*Looks around.*] It's all right, Dad. They're talking to Mr. Seward.

GAY. Fine! Now the main thing is to get the seat delivered

without your mother's seeing it. I've got to telephone Mac-Gregor—

PARKER. How much is he going to soak you?

GAY. Too much. The old skinflint was asking a hundred, but I've got him down to ninety. By the way, he doesn't know I'm me. I mean, I've kept away from him—done my bidding by telephone.

PARKER. I get you. He knows how much Momps wants that seat; if he knew who you were—

GAY. [Dialing number on telephone.] He just might put up the price.

PARKER. He's a slicker, all right.

BITS. [Comes back through French windows.] Who's a slicker?

GAY. [Hastily puts down receiver.] Nobody.

PARKER. It's a secret.

BITS. Pooh! I know a secret, too. I wouldn't tell it if you offered me a billion dollars.

PARKER. Pahdon my lawfter.

BITS. All I'll tell you is that it has four legs—and a back—and lots of horse-hair—but it isn't a horse.

PARKER. You're a dirty snooper!

GAY. Sh! [Craftily producing a quarter from his pocket.] Look here, Bitsy, we can't guess what you're talking about, but we wouldn't want your mother to get her mind fixed on this four-legged object—would we?

PARKER. You bet we wouldn't!

GAY. —So here's a quarter says you're going to keep your mouth shut.

BITS. Why, of course I will, Daddy. [*An afterthought, looking puzzled.*] About what?

PARKER. Never mind what!

GAY. You just trot along and spend your money.

BITS. Thank you, but I'm not spending my money—I'm hoarding it. [*Expands her meager little chest.*] For a Beauty-Form Build-Up Bra.

LINNY. [*Enters Left, calling back over her shoulder.*] Thanks a million! [*To* GAY.] Oh, hello! I thought you'd be ready to go downtown by now.

GAY. Well, seeing it's Saturday—and our anniversary—I've just about decided not to go down today.

LINNY. [*Blankly.*] You have!

GAY. Lots of things I could do about the house; that leaky faucet upstairs, and the garage doors. I've always been intending to fix the garage doors.

PARKER. I'll help you, Dad.

GAY. Fine! [*To his wife, with an involuntary glance toward the telephone.*] I suppose you'll be leaving for the market pretty soon?

LINNY. [*Also glancing toward telephone.*] Well, not right away. I've got the dishes to do first.

GAY. Parker and I'll do them for you.

PARKER. Sure! We'll do them, Momps.

LINNY. [*Surprised.*] Why, thank you! Then I can get right at my check book. [*Crosses to desk, picks up check book which is of the large, three-checks-to-a-page variety and is bursting with extraneous matter.*] That stupid bank's mixed my account all up again. It's a wonder they don't have some system. [*Picks up check book which immediately showers grocery slips, shopping lists, cancelled checks and vouchers all over the floor.*]

GAY. There ought to be a law about it.

[*He and* PARKER *go off into kitchen.*]

BITS. [*Who is on her knees, picking up papers.*] It's all right, Mom. You can call now.

LINNY. [*Dialing.*] I do hope he's there. [*Into telephone—all in a rush.*] Hello! Mr. MacGregor?—I've got some good news for you— I want my seat— Right away— Send it to Mr. Samuel Seward, six twenty-five Maple Drive and have the delivery man put it in the garage.

BITS. You haven't told him who you are.

LINNY. I haven't? Oh— [*Into telephone.*] This is Mrs. Gaylord Gordon— You've *what?*—But you can't sell my seat! [*To* BITS.] He says some man's bidding— [*Into telephone.*] Of course it's mine! You know I've been shopping on it for months! The only reason I didn't pay a deposit was because I didn't have the money.

BITS. [*Coaching.*] Tell him you've got it now.

LINNY. I've got the money now. I certainly have! Send the seat right over and I'll give you eighty-five dollars cash— *What?*

BITS. Not so loud!

LINNY. You distinctly told me eighty-five— Oh, *no!* [*To* BITS.] He says he's been bid a hundred! [*Into telephone again.*] I think that's a very mercenary attitude for you to take!—I do indeed!—Very well, if I must, I'll give a hundred and five. [*To* BITS.] How I'll ever scrape it up—! [*Into telephone.*] What? Well, I can't see why it's necessary, but if you've promised I suppose I'll have to wait. I *do* think you're very disobliging. Goodbye! [*Hangs up.*] He won't give me any answer 'til that dreadful man has called him.

BITS. Maybe it's somebody we know.

LINNY. I'm sure nobody we know would do such a thing— waiting all these months, then swooping down like a *vulture* the very moment I need it—

GAY. [*Enters from kitchen on cue "very." He has a dish towel tied around his waist.*] Do I pour the bacon grease down the sink?

LINNY. Goodness, no! Put it in the— Never mind. We'll finish up. [*Moves Left to take towel from* GAY *who picks up newspaper as though to read it.*] Aren't you going to get at that garage door?

GAY. It'll keep. [*Sits in the chair as though settling for the morning.*]

[LINNY *looks at him, worried, then goes into kitchen.* PARKER *comes out, wearing a fancy cretonne apron.*]

BITS. How perfectly *sweet* you look!

[*Goes past her brother into kitchen. He removes the apron, wads it in a ball and throws it after her. The instant the*

WOMEN *are out of the room* GAY *throws down paper, strides across to the telephone.*]

GAY. [*Dialing.*] Stand guard while I call. [*Into telephone.*] Hello, is this MacGregor's— Oh, good morning, Mr. Mac-Gregor. I'm the man who called yesterday about—that's right. The love-seat. I'm going to send you ninety dollars— *What?*

PARKER. Pipe down, Pop!

GAY. A hundred and fifteen!

PARKER. Don't let him put anything over on you!

GAY. He says he's had another offer. [*Into telephone.*] I don't care if it *is* from an old customer! I made you a definite proposition and— All right, if you do business that way I'll have to pay it, but I'll never— What's that?—No, you can't call me. I'll have to call you— Yes, in five minutes. Goodbye! [*Bangs receiver down on cradle.*] A hundred and fifteen for that piece of trash!

PARKER. Golly! What happened?

GAY. Some fool woman's mussing in; raising the ante.

PARKER. Say! Perhaps it's— [*A motion toward kitchen.*]

GAY. She's offering cash.

PARKER. That lets Momps out.

GAY. What burns me is her popping up right *now*. Just when I want it for our anniversary. [*His wrath rises again.*] I'll be eternally confounded if I'll let her get away with it! [*Brings fist down on desk.*]

LINNY. [*Hurrying in from kitchen.*] Did the telephone ring?

GAY. No.

PARKER. It didn't ring. } [*Together.*]

[*Telephone rings. They* BOTH *jump.* LINNY *fairly flies across room.*]

LINNY. I'll get it. [*Into telephone.*] Hello! Yes, this is Mrs. Gordon. [*Looks distractedly at* GAY.] Would you mind—er—turning off the water in the sink? I'm sure I left it running. [*Into telephone, too, too heartily.*] Why, yes, Mrs. Parkingson, I'd be delighted to serve on your committee! [*As* GAY *goes into kitchen followed by* PARKER.] Oh, Mr. MacGregor! I didn't recognize your voice— Yes, very odd!

BITS. [*Coming in from kitchen.*] You didn't leave any water running, Momps.

LINNY. Don't bother me now— No! No! Mr. MacGregor, I was speaking to my daughter. How much did he bid?—A hundred and twenty!

BITS. Twenty!

LINNY. You mean you expect me to top that?

BITS. Murder!

LINNY. [*Distractedly.*] I don't think that's fair at all!—Of course I've heard of the competitive system, but I can't see it's any excuse for raising prices!—Yes, yes, I do want the seat, but forty dollars extra—

BITS. I'll loan you my allowance.

LINNY. That's sweet of you, darling. [*Into telephone.*] Not you. I was speaking to my daughter again— A hundred and twenty-five! Oh, dear! If you'd just give me time to think— You will? Oh, thank you! If I can raise that amount I'll call you back— Yes. Goodbye! [*Hangs up, has another thought, takes receiver again.*] But I still think it's very unfair! Hello! Hello! Why, He's hung up on me!

BITS. What are you going to do now?

LINNY. [*Picks up large book labeled "Household" and sits down at desk.*] I'm going to try to squeeze forty dollars out of my budget. [*Studies account book.*] Now, let me see— not counting that overdraft—which the bank is entirely mistaken about—I've got eighty-five plus ten plus two-fifty— plus the household allowance—to run on for a month. I can't cut any more on food—and electricity and gas come out of your father.

BITS. We can't give up the cook because we haven't got one. [*A sudden inspiration.*] I know! I'll give up the dentist!

LINNY. Don't be silly. [*Sighing as she studies the account book.*] There's no two ways about it. It'll have to come out of clothing. Let me see—"Blue hat"—I don't really need another hat. That will save fifteen dollars. "Bits: Party dress"—

BITS. Momps!

LINNY. Your old one is still perfectly good.

BITS. It's perfectly infantile! And short! Up to here!

LINNY. I can drop the hem and put on some lace. Then with some pretty new ribbons—

BITS. Oh, *no!*

LINNY. I'll let you carry my vanity.

BITS. I'd ought to carry a teething-ring!

LINNY. [*Figuring on a piece of paper.*] Say fifteen for the hat—and twenty-five for the dress—

BITS. But that strapless, backless model at the Emporium's only fourteen ninety-five.

LINNY. That wouldn't make it come out right, dear. By *not* buying a fifteen dollar hat and a twenty-five dollar dress I'll save exactly forty dollars.

BITS. [*Letting down her blouse at the top and looking wistfully at the effect in the mirror over the desk.*] That strapless, backless model is breathtakingly beautiful.

LINNY. Then it's just as well you can't have it. You need your breath. Two, five, seventeen—

BITS. [*Slowly, working out an idea.*] Momps, if I were to tell you something, do you think I'd have to give back the quarter I got for not mentioning it to you?

LINNY. [*Absently.*] If I ever meet that man I'll strangle him! [*A delayed reaction.*] Who paid you for not mentioning what?

BITS. Daddy. That love-seat. He said he didn't want you getting your mind on it.

LINNY. He did!

BITS. [*A young Machiavelli.*] That kind of looks as though he doesn't like it—don't you think?

LINNY. It does. It certainly does!

BITS. I guess maybe it'd be better if you didn't buy it, after all.

LINNY. Yes—no— Oh dear, now I *am* confused. If he really dislikes it—but how am I going to find out?

BITS. You could hint around, couldn't you?

LINNY. I suppose I could. Yes, I'll bring up the subject casually. We'll see how he reacts.

BITS. Mm. Dad's an awfully good reactionary—

[LINNY *moves toward hall as* PARKER *comes in cautiously from kitchen.*]

LINNY. In the meantime we'd better take a look at your dress.

BITS. Seems as if I've been looking at it for the last ten years!

[*They are off.* PARKER *crosses the room in two jumps, dials a number, speaks in a low voice.*]

PARKER. Hello, is this Mr. —er— It is? Well, I'm calling for the gentleman about that—uh—you know—it costs a hundred and fifteen— [*A shout.*] *What?*

GAY. [*Coming in from kitchen.*] What's the matter?

PARKER. The ole pirate's jacked the price up to a hundred and thirty!

GAY. A hundred and—

PARKER. Says that dame's bidding one-twenty-five. [*Into telephone.*] But it's practically junk! You'd ought to pay for having it hauled away!

GAY. [*Anxiously.*] Wait! [*Takes receiver, listens to a tirade from the other end.*] Yes, Mr. MacGregor— No, Mr. MacGregor—I didn't say I wouldn't pay it. When I sit in a game, no female's going to bluff me out!

PARKER. Go slow, Dad!

GAY. Whatever she's offered I'll raise her five, but I'm calling for a show-down. I want that seat delivered now—at once!—I don't give a continental damn what you told her! I'm topping her bid! Deliver it to—

PARKER. Wait! I got an idea! [*Takes receiver from* GAY.] Deliver it to the garage back of six twenty-five Maple Drive —yes—to Mr. Samuel Seward— [*To* GAY.] Mr. Seward won't mind. We'll have a chance to clean 'er up.

GAY. Fine! [*Takes back receiver.*] If it isn't here in twenty minutes, so help me Harry, I'll sick the Better Business Bureau onto you!

PARKER. [*Into mouthpiece.*] And the F.B.I.!

GAY. Goodbye! [*Hangs up with a bang.*]

PARKER. That's tellin' 'em!

GAY. Now all we've got to do is get rid of your mother.

PARKER. Leave her to me! [*At door into hall, calling off.*] Hey, Momps, how's about me driving you down to market?

LINNY. [*Off.*] Not right now, thanks, dear.

PARKER. If you wait any longer all the food'll be gone.

LINNY. [*Off.*] Then we'll just have to starve.

[*The two men stare at each other.*]

GAY. H'm!

PARKER. Don't you think she's acting kind of funny?

GAY. Funny is right.

PARKER. It's like she was beginning to suspect about—you know.

GAY. Well, if she has any suspicions I'll murder 'em—but quick! I started out to surprise her and, by Jupiter, she's going to be surprised if I have to—

PARKER. [*On cue "if I"*] Holy Cow!

[GAY *swings around, discovers* PARKER *is staring at something beyond the hall door. This proves to be* BITS, *dressed in her party dress. She was right, when she said it was short. It is also tight, the waist line almost up to her armpits.*]

LINNY. [*Entering behind her.*] I tell you it doesn't look bad on you at all, does it, Daddy?

PARKER. Bad! ⎫
GAY. What's happened to it? ⎬ [*Together.*]

BITS. [*Ready to weep.*] It hasn't happened to *it*. It's happened to *me!*

LINNY. She's grown. But I can fix the hem and let out the waist. The dress really isn't so old, dear.

BITS. Old! It's practically an *antique!*

LINNY AND GAY. [*Together, as though the word is a trigger which has set them off.*] Speaking of antiques— [BOTH *stop, then speak again.*]

LINNY. Excuse me— ⎫
GAY. You first— ⎬ [*Together.*]

LINNY. What was I—? Oh, yes! [*Fakes elaborate unconcern by dusting desk with handkerchief.*] I happened to pass

MacGregor's Antique Shop yesterday. I noticed that love-seat was missing.

GAY. [*Vaguely; picking up newspaper.*] Love-seat? Oh, yes —the love-seat.

PARKER. [*Wide-eyed.*] What's a love-seat, Dad?

GAY. It's a sawed-off sofa.

BITS. It used to be in his corner window.

PARKER. [*Giving it everything.*] You mean that moldy old thing with the stuffing coming out?

GAY. The legs were falling off, too.

BITS. [*Aside to her mother.*] What'd I tell you?

LINNY. Sh! [*Casually, again.*] I wonder what Mr. Mac-Gregor did with it?

GAY. Probably chopped it up for firewood.

PARKER. Or fed it to the termites.

LINNY. [*Pathetically to* GAY.] I thought at one time you rather liked it.

GAY. Liked it?

PARKER. Whatever gave you that idea?

GAY. I thought it a bit revolting. [LINNY *chokes and hurries Left.*] What's the matter, dear?

LINNY. Nothing! Nothing at all!

BITS. [*Following her off into kitchen.*] Can't I take this off now, Momps?

GAY. Well, we lulled her suspicions, all right!

PARKER. Just hit 'em on the head with a little ole meat-axe!

GAY. [*Sitting down at desk.*] Keep an eye out for that delivery truck while I write a check— [*Starts to push aside notes written earlier by* LINNY, *suddenly looks closer; bursts out*s] My soul and body!

PARKER. Huh?

GAY. Take a look at this!

PARKER. [*Reading.*] "Cash in hand, eighty-five. Saved on hat, fifteen. Ditto dress, Bits, twenty-five—" [*Eyes follow his father's pointing finger.*] "L. seat a hundred and twenty-five." It *was* Momps!

GAY. And nobody else!

PARKER. The dame that ran up the price on you!

GAY. Made me bid my fool head off!

PARKER. Quick, Dad! Get MacGregor on the phone—

GAY. Not me! I'm going to take it up with him face to face!

PARKER. That I want to see!

GAY. Then come on!

LINNY. [*Entering from kitchen.*] Where are you going?

GAY. To visit a sick friend.

PARKER. Anyway, he's *going* to be sick.

LINNY. [*Staring after them as they go off through hall.*] Well, upon my word!

BITS. [*Running in from kitchen.*] Momps! Momps! There's an expressman next door. He's delivering the you-know-what.

LINNY. [*Hurrying Left.*] He can't be! I haven't phoned yet— [*At French windows.*] Why, there it is!

BITS. I told you! He's carrying it back to the garage.

LINNY. Stop him! Mr. Expressman! Wait! Mr. Expressman!

JOE. [*Off.*] You call me?

LINNY. Yes, please— [*To* BITS.] Oh, dear—I don't want your father to see— [*To* EXPRESSMAN *again.*] Don't leave that there!

[JOE, *a typical hardboiled delivery man, appears in the windows. He has the love-seat precariously balanced on a wheeled truck. It is a rare object—or was about seventy-five years ago. The world since then has been hard on it.*]

JOE. The laugh's sure on me. I thought next door was number six twenty-five.

BITS. It is.

JOE. Is it? [*Gets a look at her costume and almost drops the love-seat off the truck—recovers from his shock with difficulty.*] It—uh—is?

LINNY. I called you to say that I don't want that love-seat.

JOE. [*Looks at address tag, then at her.*] You Mr. Samuel Seward?

LINNY. Of course not.

JOE. Then you ain't got a worry. I'm delivering this to Mr. Samuel Seward.

BITS. We know.

JOE. Six twenty-five Maple Drive.

LINNY. You're delivering it to me.

JOE. You bought it?

LINNY. No, I didn't buy it—

JOE. Then everything's hunky-dory. If you'll just stand to one side—I'll finish my delivering.

LINNY. But I don't want it delivered!

JOE. [*Holding on to himself.*] Lady—tell me. Do you live next door?

LINNY. No. I live here.

JOE. And I ain't deliverin' it here. I'm deliverin' it next door.

LINNY. But I've told you I didn't buy it!

JOE. [*Soothingly—as he tries to slip the love-seat toward the French windows.*] Sure you didn't. That's why I'm not deliverin' it to you—because you didn't buy it—see?

BITS. But she was going to buy it.

JOE. Huh?

LINNY. And while I thought I was going to I told Mr. Mac-Gregor to deliver it over there because I didn't want Mr. Gordon to see it over here.

JOE. [*Beginning to go to pieces.*] You didn't want—Say! How'd this Gordon character get into it?

BITS. He's my father.

LINNY. I'm Mrs. Gordon.

JOE. [*Absently tipping his hat.*] Pleased to meecha.

LINNY. I asked Mr. MacGregor to deliver this to Mr. Seward because it was our anniversary.

BITS. They've been married eighteen years.

JOE. You and Mr. Seward?

LINNY. Me and Mr.—Mr. Gordon and *I*. I planned to sneak over to Mr. Seward's without my husband's knowing— [JOE *glances at* BITS. LINNY *catches the glance, speaks quickly.*] Mr. Seward's a very old friend.

JOE. Sure! Sure!

LINNY. But then something made me feel my husband wouldn't like it.

BITS. [*Brightly to* JOE.] So that's why Mother didn't buy the seat.

JOE. [*Sunk without a trace.*] Oh, it is!

LINNY. Yes. Bits, go watch for your father. [*To* JOE *as* BITS *skips Right into hall.*] He mustn't find you here.

JOE. I'll say—

LINNY. If you'd like me to explain again—

JOE. Lady—rather than you should go through that again I would take back twenty seats!

[*He is wearily trundling the truck Left as* BITS *flies back in from the hall.*]

BITS. Jigger!

LINNY. [*Pushing* JOE *and the truck toward the windows.*] Oh, hurry! Hurry!

GAY. [*Comes in with* PARKER.] Hey!

PARKER. Wait a minute!

GAY. Bring that back! It's mine!

LINNY. Gay!

JOE. You Mr. Seward?

GAY. I'm Mr. Gordon.

JOE. [*A glance toward* LINNY *and* BITS.] You sure got my sympathy.

GAY. [*Misunderstanding.*] Oh, she won't be so bad when she's re-covered and got her legs fixed.

JOE. Huh? [*Sees* GAY *is looking at the love-seat.*] You tellin' me you bought it?

GAY. No, I didn't buy it.

PARKER. He swopped for it.

LINNY. Darling!⎫
⎬ [*Together.*]
BITS. Swopped!⎭

GAY. Our old lawn-mower—plus fifty dollars.

LINNY. And that awful man offered him a hundred and— [*An idea stops her short.*] Gay!

GAY. [*Quickly.*] We won't go into that!

BITS. But, Daddy—

JOE. Okay! Okay! I can't hold this forever. Where you want it?

LINNY. Over here— ⎫   [*Together. Pointing*
GAY. Over there— ⎬ *in opposite directions.*]

JOE. You're going to get it *here*—[*Dumps seat in middle of floor, facing upstage.*]—and like it!

LINNY. [*Gazes gloatingly at the horrific thing.*] Oh! It's even more beautiful than I remembered it!

BITS. [*To* LINNY *and* GAY.] Sit on it!

PARKER. We want to see how you look.

BITS. Show us how you used to canoodle!

GAY. [*Arm around his wife.*] Come on, honey.

[*The two swing around to sit on the seat which is still standing, its high, solid back to the audience. There is a sound of ripping upholstery. Several springs fly into the air. A front leg gives way. Both* GAY *and* LINNY *disappear from view. The* CHILDREN *shout with laughter.*]

JOE. [*Saluting.*] Happy anniversary! [*He starts out with the truck.*]

CURTAIN